KARMA AND REBIRTH

Karma
and
Rebirth

CHRISTMAS HUMPHREYS

CURZON
PRESS

Published in 1994 by
Curzon Press Ltd.
St John's Studios
Church Road
Richmond
Surrey TW9 2QA

Reprinted 2002 by RoutledgeCurzon
11 New Fetter Lane,
London EC4P 4EE

RoutledgeCurzon is an imprint of the Taylor & Francis Group

© Curzon Press 1994

British Library Cataloguing-in-Publication data
A CIP record for this title is
available from the British Library

ISBN 0 7007 0163 X

Printed in Great Britain by
Bookcraft, Bath

Preface to New Edition

Karma and Rebirth was first published in 1943, at a time when the Second World War was at its height. The doctrine, known to the East from time immemorial, was new to the West, and the effect of its acceptance on those grieving for their loved ones was immense. The news of someone's death, from a wound of cold finality, was seen as only the premature happening of an event which is periodic for us all.

If love is indeed 'the fulfilling of the law' the force of these twin aspects of the nameless Absolute, which the Buddha called 'the Unborn', will surely, in a life as yet to come, heal the apparent severance.

But today it seems that the twin doctrine is helping an ever-widening public to drop the fear of death, to see that justice rules the world and all within it, and that we are indeed, in the smallest detail, at least potential masters of our destiny.

1983   T.C.H.

Contents

Introduction

There are many books on the twin doctrines of Karma and Rebirth, but the tendency of each new publication is to present the subject as more and more mechanical, until so nearly does this timeless, universal Law approximate to a soulless Fate that what is in fact a reign of law becomes a reign of terror, and compassion, described in *The Voice of the Silence* as 'the Law of Laws, eternal Harmony', is utterly ignored. The cause of this degradation is probably twofold; first, the general tendency of Western thought to materialize whatever spiritual principles swim into its ken, and secondly, the increasing departure from the available sources of our knowledge of the doctrine, with the corresponding reliance of each writer on previous textbooks and his own ideas.

In the result, most Western writers on the subject confine themselves to the 'lower knowledge' described by the Vedanta philosophers, which is sufficient for those too lazy to awaken in themselves the higher centres from which alone the 'higher knowledge' may be seen. But though the law of Karma must, on its own plane, remain to us unknowable, a thoughtful study of the sources from which our knowledge is derived will give the genuine student a vision of essential principles which, if not yet of the 'higher knowledge' reserved for the few, may serve to awaken the higher centres through which, as windows on to the Absolute, the Truth may finally be known.

The present volume is therefore a humble attempt to reconsider the subject in the light of such 'authorities' as are available and from a more spiritual and therefore less mechanical point of view. The doctrine is too old and too widely held to be regarded as the property of any one religion, but the Scriptures of the Hindus and Buddhists provide the oldest available sources. When to these are added, by way of commentary, the writings of H. P. Blavatsky, who was herself trained in Tibetan monasteries, there is available a triple 'authority' which, taken as a whole provides the basis for an all-embracing Law which guides and governs the evolution of mankind.

Yet the ultimate authority for any doctrine is not in the written nor in the spoken word, but rather in its own sweet reasonableness, and in the fact that it is ratified by the intuition and seems to 'work out' in the day's experience. Neither God nor man may prove to another that a principle is true. As the Buddha said to the Kalamas: 'Do not go by hearsay, nor by what is handed down by others, nor by what people say, nor by what is stated on the authority of your traditional teachings . . . But, Kalamas, when you know of yourselves: "These teachings are good; these teachings, when followed out and put into practice, conduce to the ending of suffering, to peace of mind, to Nirvana"—then accept them.'

In accordance with this view of authority, no authority

is claimed for the views of the writers quoted in this essay, and therefore no exact references have been given. Where, however, another's words express my meaning better or more cogently than my own, I have adopted them for the reader's benefit. For the rest, there is no authority for any man save the 'still small voice' within.

It is an axiom, approved by all experience, that the more spiritual a doctrine the more is it immediately applicable in daily life, and in presenting Karma and Rebirth against their spiritual background they will be found to be of more immediate application than when regarded as a mere mechanical debit and credit account in the ledgers of some extra-cosmic God. I therefore write in no sense as a scholar, nor as one presenting an interesting belief of the Orient. Rather I write as one who believes the doctrine to be true, and believes that any reconstruction of Western civilization is doomed to failure unless it is based on conscious co-operation with this ultimate and all-embracing Law. As Loftus Hare wrote:[1] 'A man becomes what he does. Can this doctrine be refuted? If it be true it is the most important and the most neglected truth in the world.' One might add, that if it be false it is strange that none has yet attempted to prove its falsity, nor offered a better solution of the 'Riddle of Life'.

But because it is true the doctrine is intensely difficult. Those who imagine that the fundamental truths of

[1] *Mysticism of East and West.*

11

existence can be described on the plane of the intellect have yet to discover that these tremendous principles are not facts, as pebbles on the beach are facts, but cosmic forces compared with which the power and grandeur of the Niagara Falls are insignificant. In the *Brihad Upanishad*, one of the oldest Hindu Scriptures, Karma is referred to as 'a mighty secret', which only the initiated may know. In the *Sutta Nipata*, one of the oldest Buddhist Scriptures, Ananda says of Karma to the Blessed One, 'How deep is this Causal Law, and how deep it seems! And yet do I regard it as quite plain to understanding.' To which the Buddha replied, 'Say not so, Ananda, say not so! Deep indeed is this Causal Law, and deep it appears to be. It is by not knowing, by not understanding, by not penetrating this doctrine that the world of men has become entangled like a ball of twine . . . unable to pass beyond the Way of Woe, and the ceaseless round of Rebirth.' Even to our intelligence the ramifications and interrelations of cause and effect in all the departments of the Universe are so immensely complex that none would presume to understand them; how infinitely more enlightened must that being be whose understanding can embrace this Law at the fountain head of its eternal majesty!

Only by studying, and to some extent grasping, an outline of the Wisdom of which Karma and Rebirth are part can the meanest vision of the doctrine be attained, and even then it is difficult to examine it apart from the

Wisdom itself from which, as sunlight in the air, it is inseparable. Yet the difficulty is largely of our own making. For centuries the Western mind has been building up an utterly false notion of a separate 'I', and it is hard for us to grasp a view of existence in which the separative self is viewed as an illusion and the father of all suffering. It follows, whether or not the idea be pleasing to the scholar mind, that only he who treads the Way which leads to the end of separative self-hood will attain to understanding of the Wisdom wherein self, as something separate, can have no abiding-place.

Study, deep study, quiet meditation on the living principles revealed in that study, and the constant, self-regardless application of those principles to daily life, these alone will provide the final 'proof' of the laws of Karma and Rebirth, and only he who knows them thus will be in a position to offer to the West, by the written and the spoken word and by the force of character, the Wisdom of which the West has so abundant and so urgent need.

C. H.

I

The Law of Karma

The word Karma, or in its neuter form, *Karman* (in Pali,
Kamma), is a Sanskrit word from the root *kri*, meaning to
do or to make. Karma is therefore 'doing' or 'making',
but in the course of time the word has been applied to
what Lessing has described as the oldest doctrine in the
world. It may be viewed exoterically, from the material
point of view, in which case it is merely the law of
causation, the balance of cause and effect, the fact known
in every science laboratory that action and reaction are
equal and opposite. Esoterically, from the spiritual point
of view, Karma is the law of moral retribution, whereby
not only does every cause have an effect, but he who puts
the cause in action suffers the effect. Professor Radhakrishnan has called it 'the law of the conservation of moral
energy'. It is magnificently described in the eighth book
of the *Light of Asia*, one stanza of which must here
suffice.

That which ye sow ye reap. See yonder fields!
　The sesamum was sesamum, the corn
Was corn. The Silence and the Darkness knew!
　So is a man's fate born.

15

The Law of Karma

This law of merit and demerit, Karma in the sense of
the reign of moral law, is neither particularly Hindu,
Buddhist nor Theosophical. It is fundamental in all
Oriental philosophy, and was preached by St. Paul.
'Brethren, be not deceived. God is not mocked, for what-
soever a man soweth that shall he also reap.' For the first
few centuries of Christianity it remained a cardinal belief
in the West. But at the Council of Constantinople, in
A.D. 551, the Christian Fathers, finding the doctrine of
Rebirth incompatible with the curious system of thought
which they were in the process of creating, decided that
belief in Rebirth should be henceforth anathema, and
with this doctrine went that which makes it necessary of
acceptance, Karma. Now, under the double influence of
English translations of the Hindu and Buddhist Scriptures,
and the reproclaiming by Mme Blavatsky of the Ancient
Wisdom, or Theosophy, of which all religions are part,
Karma and Rebirth have returned to the West, and a
glance at chapter VII of this book will show to what a
wide extent the dual doctrine has proved acceptable.

Either it is true or false. The Universe is either cosmos
or chaos, for it cannot be partly ruled by law and partly
by a blind, unreasonable chance. Karma is not a law of
which it can be said: 'There may be something in it.'
Either the Law exists or it does not. If it exists he is a
fool who does not use it, and he alone is wise who studies
it, proclaims it far and wide, and applies it to the smallest
detail of his daily life. If it be not true it is a strangely

16

venerable error, and seeing that it has been taught as the basis of the world's accumulated wisdom since, it would seem, the search for truth began, it is strange that no other Law has been propounded to explain this life's pheno- mena. But the Law is only understandable from the spiritual point of view. To regard it as a mechanical law of debit and credit for good and evil actions is to rob the doctrine of its living power. If it is all-embracing, coeval with the Universe, it can only be grasped from a universal, that is to say, a spiritual point of view. Man has many levels of cognition, windows on the spiral staircase of his understanding, and even as the lighthouse-keeper, whose tower is based in the living rock, climbs to the level of the lantern where he tends the light which is not *his* light, so man's evolving consciousness must climb from plane to plane until he finds, and learns to tend, the Light within, which shines eternally. Beyond the intellect, which is the machinery of thought, is the plane of the intuition, the faculty of immediate, direct cognition of Reality. In most of us it sleeps, or functions dimly in a low reflection as the 'instincts', or on the psychic plane. Yet all may develop it, and none may know the Law who has not to some extent acquired it as an active instrument. At first it serves to illumine the intellect with fitful flashes of under- standing; later, the ascending consciousness begins to use it on its own plane, and he who has experienced such daz- zling glimpses of 'the heart of things' will know, and know beyond all doubting, that the Law is true. Meanwhile, on the level of the intellect, where doubts arise and cloud the understanding, the Law can only be viewed as a doctrine of sweet reasonableness which, in the workshops of experience, is tested and found true. Karma is a Law, a Law which dominates all other natural laws, from gravity to the law of averages, but it is not blind Law. It is living and intelligent as all else in the Universe. 'There is no such thing as either "dead" or "blind" matter, as there is no "blind" or "unconscious" Law', for

the Universe is worked and guided from within outwards. As above so it is below, as in heaven so on earth; and man, the microcosm and miniature copy of the macrocosm, is the living witness to this Universal Law, and to the mode of its action.[1]

The Wisdom-Religion

From this it must be obvious that in order to understand Karma it is necessary to have some knowledge of the Wisdom of which it is the basic law. Only then will it be seen as a necessary part of the cosmic Whole, and the place of man, the law-giver who is yet subject to the law, made clear. This Wisdom-Religion, older than any known religion, will be found to be based upon three fundamental Principles. These are necessarily difficult to describe, first because they speak of things which lie beyond the range of our limited intelligence, secondly because any description involves the use of words and

[1] *The Secret Doctrine*, H. P. Blavatsky.

names, and both are widely different in the various descriptions of the Principles, and thirdly because any attempt to define and describe such cosmic Laws is like picking up a handful of a rushing stream or attempting to pigeon-hole the tide.

The Ultimate Principle, which all the capital letters in the alphabet can never describe, is the Parabrahman of the Hindus, the Adi Buddha of the Mahayana Buddhists, the Fana-al-Fana of the Sufis, and the Tao, in its highest sense, of the Taoists. It is, in the words of *The Secret Doctrine*,

an Omnipresent, Eternal, Boundless and Immutable PRIN-CIPLE, on which all speculation is impossible, since it transcends the power of human conception and can only be dwarfed by any human expression or similitude. It is beyond the range and reach of thought.

It is, as the writer later says, 'Be-ness' rather than Being, and many prefer to consider it as the ultimate Nameless-ness. It is important to note further that 'its impersonality is the fundamental conception of the System', and that it is therefore utterly beyond the limited and limiting belief in a personal God. 'It is latent in every atom of the Universe, and is the Universe itself.'

But 'Be-ness', to be recognizable to itself, must manifest, and the manifested Universe is the Field of Becoming whereon the One unrolls into the Many and returns again. This periodic 'rolling and unrolling', as the Buddhist Scriptures call it, occupies immense though not,

19

it is said, incalculable periods of time. It demonstrates 'the universality of that law of periodicity, of flux and reflux, ebb and flow, which physical science has observed and recorded in all departments of nature', and which is contained in the Buddhist doctrine of *anicca*, ceaseless change. The Universe when manifest is but of relative Reality, or Maya, yet deep in the heart of each of the Many is a fragment or ray of the One, and each human mind is an aspect or ray of the Universal Mind—the 'Essence of Mind' of the *Sutra of Wei Lang*—which is the 'appearance' of the Namelessness. Within this Field of Becoming the One has become Two. But no two things are cognizable without relationship, and with this relationship the Two become Three.

From Three in turn comes Seven, and from the Seven come what the Chinese call the Ten Thousand Things, the manifested Universe in its infinite diversity. The fundamental 'Pair of Opposites' is Spirit and Matter, Subject and Object, the Purusha and Prakriti of Indian philosophy, and from the interplay of this original duality is spun on the warp of motive and the woof of acts, the Karma which we create and suffer, create and suffer as the Wheel of Becoming turns unceasingly.

The third Fundamental Principle is sometimes called the Cycle of Necessity, the necessary pilgrimage of every 'soul' (using that term as the ray of the Flame in every man), from purest 'Spirit' into darkest 'Matter' and then, on the return journey, 'home'. Within this mighty cycle of one complete unrolling and re-rolling of the Universe there are, of course, an infinity of lesser cycles. Even on this earth, itself subject to cosmic cycles of birth and death, there are tremendous cycles, from those which belong to the field of geology to those which affect the mass migration and the racial cycles of men. Ever the cycle runs—'Coming to be, coming to be; ceasing to be, ceasing to be'[1]—or, in greater detail, birth, growth, decay and death; birth, growth, decay and death.

In the Buddhist Scriptures this cycle is still further analysed into the twelve Nidanas, which Mme Blavatsky describes as a detailed expression of the Law of Karma under twelve aspects. The subject is more fully treated in Mme David-Neel's *Buddhism, its Doctrines and Methods* and in *What is Buddhism?*[2] and need not be elaborated here. These twelve spokes of the 'Wheel of Causation', however, do throw light on the process of involution and evolution, according as they are read forwards or in inverse order, and are essential for those who desire to study the 'rolling and unrolling' of the Universe. It is important to note that the spokes are not merely causal, i.e. directly sequential the one from the other, but form an elaborate interrelation of causal factors on all planes. The first is Jaramarana, old age and death, for life is cradled in death; every atom, as soon as it is born, begins to die. Old age and death is therefore caused by Jati, birth.

[1] From the *Sutta Nipata.*
[2] Compiled and published by the Buddhist Lodge, London.

'The cause of death is birth.' Birth is caused by Bhava, 'becoming', which is the Karmic agent of rebirth, and Bhava is caused by Upadana, fierce attachment to life and the things of life which man, in his ignorance, foolishly believes will quench his 'thirst', or Tanha (Sanskrit, Trishna), the desire for sentient existence. This thirst or desire is caused by Vedana, feelings, which is in turn produced by Phassa, contact, the connecting link between the organs of sense and the objects they cognize. Contact comes through the six senses, Sparsha, being the usual five and the lower mind, and these arise from Nama-Rupa, literally Name and Form. The cause of Nama-Rupa is Vinnana, consciousness which, needing a vehicle for self-expression, creates for itself a 'meaning and form' through which it manifests. Consciousness in turn is the outcome of the Sankharas, about which volumes might be written, for these compounds of thoughts, belief, ideals and prejudices together form 'the germs of propensities and impulses from previous births to be developed in this', and as such are an aspect of Karma itself. But Karma in this sense is the product of Avidya, ignorance, the dark illusion which is the womb of suffering and the basis of causation and its endless progeny of cause-effects.

The Nature of Man

What, then, is the place of man in this mighty scheme of things?

Man is a complex entity, and whether he be regarded

as the 'spirit, soul and body' of St Paul, or as the more complex analysis of Indian philosophy, which ignores both the physical body and the spirit and yet leaves five other planes of consciousness, or whether the number be carried to seven, as set out in the Ancient Wisdom itself, is a matter of terminology and choice. For the purpose of this account of Karma and Rebirth the Pauline analysis will suffice. Man *is* spirit, that is to say, he is of the very essence of that 'Be-ness' which is 'beyond the range and reach of thought', and the various 'garments' which he wears are the vehicles or instruments through which he contacts the descending planes of consciousness. These bodies or instruments are all made of 'matter', but of matter which at the highest is so fine as to be all but non-existent, and at the lowest is of our 'common clay'. All alike are *anatta*, that is to say, lacking a permanent life as such, and all are *anicca*, subject to change. They change with every act at any level of consciousness, for every new cause must modify to some extent the sum total of effects which is that vehicle. It follows that the ultimate heresy, the profoundest error in all human belief, is Attavada, the belief in the essential separateness of any of these vehicles, be it mind or soul or spirit itself, from the Namelessness or infinite SELF of which all manifestation is part. This fundamental principle, the very basis for the solidarity and hence the 'brotherhood' of man, must be thoroughly grasped and assimilated before the law of Karma can be in any way understood.

The Law of Karma

We must not lose sight of the fact that every atom is subject to the general law governing the whole body to which it belongs. . . . The aggregate of individual Karma becomes that of the nation to which those individuals belong, and the sum total of National Karma is that of the world. The evils that a man suffers are not peculiar to the individual or even to the nation, they are more or less universal; and it is upon this broad line of human interdependence that the law of Karma finds its legitimate and equable issue.[1]

From this the writer proceeds to one of the finest passages in all her writings.

It is an occult law, moreover, that no man can rise superior to his individual failings without lifting, be it ever so little, the whole body of which he is an integral part. In the same way no one can sin, nor suffer the effects of sin, alone. In reality, there is no such thing as 'Separateness'; and the nearest approach to that selfish state which the laws of life permit is in the intent or motive.[1]

But if no man's spirit is separate, in that being one with the Namelessness it is not even *his*, the soul is even less immortal, for it is changing every moment of the day. It is, as will be explained later, equivalent to character, the collection of attributes, good and bad, which make up the man. Still more impermanent is the 'body', using the word in the sense of the mask or personality through which the soul, and through the soul the spirit, is made manifest.

[1] *The Key to Theosophy*, H. P. Blavatsky.

24

This outward and visible aspect of the man is the densest of his vehicles, being that through which he contacts the lowest planes of matter, yet, said the Buddha, 'In this very body, six feet in length, with its sense-impressions and its thoughts and ideas, I declare to you are the world, the origin of the world and the ceasing of the world, and likewise the Way that leads to the ceasing thereof'.[1] It follows that he who waits for a heaven-world in which to begin his inner development will wait in vain. At page 122 of Dr Jacobi's *Psychology of C. G. Jung*, there is a diagram of what that famous psychologist, as the result of a life's work, believes to be the content of the invisible side of Man. To equate the analysed aspects of man as taught by Eastern philosophy with the empirically discovered equivalents in Western psychology is a task which probably only a Dr Jung could at the moment undertake, but those who meditate upon the respective analyses will learn a vast amount from the comparison. In either case the teaching is insistent on the indivisible wholeness of the thing we know as man. Whether his 'skins' be compared to those of an onion, which may be successively removed, or his consciousness be compared to that of a lighthouse-keeper, as in the analogy used above, or the various aspects be built into a glyph or diagram, ever the SELF and all its vehicles is One, even as Karma is One, for both are subject to and aspects of the 'Be-ness' without name.

[1] *The Anguttara Nikaya.*

The Law of Karma

The Law of Equilibrium

For the study of Karma it is best to consider the man at the level of his individuality or 'soul'. Here the Self creates, uses, suffers and in a very real sense *is* its Karma, and those who study Jung's diagram will note with interest that this Self unites the most outward and most inward, most material and most spiritual parts of the whole. For the keynote of the law of Karma is equilibrium, and nature is always working to restore that equilibrium whenever through man's acts it is disturbed. As Emerson wrote,

If you love and serve men, you cannot by any hiding or stratagem escape the remuneration. Secret retributions are always restoring the level, when disturbed, of the divine justice. It is impossible to tilt the beam. All the tyrants and proprietors and monopolists of the world in vain set their shoulders to heave the bar. Settles for evermore the ponderous equator to its line, and man and mote, and star and sun must range to it, or be pulverized by the recoil.[1]

To the same effect wrote H. P. Blavatsky:

The only decree of Karma, an eternal and immutable decree, is absolute Harmony in the world of Matter as in the world of Spirit. It is not, therefore, Karma that rewards or punishes, but it is we who reward and punish ourselves, according as we work with and through Nature, abiding by the laws on which that harmony depends, or breaking them.[2]

[1] *Lectures and Biographical Sketches*, 1868.   [2] *The Secret Doctrine*.

And this in turn was echoed by W. Q. Judge, her pupil, when he wrote, in his famous *Karmic Aphorisms*, 'Karma is an undeviating and unerring tendency in the Universe to restore equilibrium, and it operates incessantly.' Because this ceaseless effort to adjust a troubled harmony takes time, the doctrine of Rebirth is a necessary corollary of Karma, for the longest life on earth will not suffice to restore the harmony disturbed by a daily round of self-regarding actions; life after life must pass before the ultimate lesson is learned, and the 'triple fires' of hatred, lust and illusion die for want of fuelling.

Karma is the master Law of the Universe, but there is no Law-giver. Its Ultimate Cause, as the ultimate cause of anything, is of course unknown and to our intelligence unknowable, but it is certainly not 'God', as the Church which claims the name of Christianity conceives that term. Absolute Consciousness, or Adi-Buddha, however one may name the Namelessness, is as far beyond the conception of a personal God as the sea is greater than a stream. The anthropomorphic God is only, as Colonel Olcott wrote, 'a gigantic shadow thrown upon the void of space by the imagination of ignorant men',[1] for even as 'the Tao that can be talked about is not the eternal Tao,' so

a man can have no God that is not bounded by his own human conceptions. The wider the sweep of his spiritual vision, the mightier will be his deity. But where can we find a better

[1] *A Buddhist Catechism.*

demonstration of Him than in man himself—in the spiritual and divine powers lying dormant in every human being? [1]

The Law is all-embracing. As is said in one of the most famous passages in the *Dhammapada*, 'Not in the sky, not in the midst of the sea, not if we enter into the clefts of the mountains, is there known a spot in the whole world where a man may be freed from an evil deed.' None is above the Law save he who has attained, by his use of the Law, supreme enlightenment, and then only because, with the dissolution of the Self which caused the Law to be set in motion, there is no longer an object on which the Law can operate.

The Law is timeless, therefore, in that it will last for as long as there remains a single being in whom it can and must inhere. Its patience is inexhaustible—

> Times are as nought, to-morrow it will judge,
> Or after many days.

Such is the Law, and it is the basis of all truth. As Paracelsus wrote, 'Philosophy is only the true perception and understanding of Cause and Effect.'

[1] *Isis Unveiled*, H. P. Blavatsky.

II

Karma in Action

Karma creates nothing.

Karma creates nothing, nor does it design. It is man who plans and creates Causes, and Karmic Law adjusts the effects, which adjustment is not an act, but universal harmony, tending ever to resume its original position, like a bough which, bent down too forcibly, rebounds with corresponding vigour.[1]

It is man who creates his Karma, for it is the product of his thought. As is written in the most famous verse in the *Dhammapada*, 'All that we are is the result of what we have thought; it is founded on our thoughts, it is made up of our thoughts.' Note the corollary which follows, when harmony demands the corresponding effect.

If a man speaks or acts with an evil thought, pain follows him, as the wheel follows the foot of him who draws the carriage. But if a man speaks or acts with a pure thought, happiness follows him, like a shadow that never leaves him.

It is of great importance to grasp the fundamental fact, as expressed by W. Q. Judge in *The Ocean of Theosophy*, that 'No act is performed without a thought at its root,

---

[1] *The Secret Doctrine*, H. P. Blavatsky.

either at the time of performance or as leading to it'. According to Indian philosophy, the sequence is ignorance, desire, will, thought and act. First comes Avidya, Ignorance, because all manifestation, and all that proceeds within it, is unenlightened. In his ignorance man desires things for himself, believing that he has a 'self' which has interests of its own. 'Man is altogether formed of desire; according as his desire is, so is his will; according as his will is, so are his deeds; according as are his deeds, so does it befall him.'[1] But between the will to act and the act is thought, the conception within the mind of which the act is the visible expression. It follows that control of thought, with which is included emotion, is a necessary prelude to control of action, for, as a man thinks, so he becomes.

Thus man, as spirit, as the highest self-conscious aspect of the One Life, rules the Universe with the aid of Karma. But once he has created Karma, as he does with every act, he must necessarily bow the knee to the Nemesis of his creation, and it is not for him to complain that Fate, against his will, has bound his actions or decreed an unjust doom. 'Karma-Nemesis is no more than the spiritual dynamical effect of causes produced and forces awakened into activity by our own actions.'[2] The higher the plane from which the harmony of nature is disturbed, the more powerful the reaction to the act.

[1] *The Brihad Upanishad.*
[2] *The Secret Doctrine,* H. P. Blavatsky.

It is a law of Occult dynamics that a given amount of energy expended on the spiritual or astral planes is productive of far greater results than the same amount expended on the physical, objective plane of existence.[1]

The Law of Karma, therefore, is utterly impersonal, being the servant of its creator, man, and not the whim of a benevolent or avenging God. It follows that it is useless to attempt to placate it, pray to it, argue with it or defy it; for 'as a man thinks, so he becomes'.

Karmic Agents

Yet it is, be it emphasized, supremely intelligent, and it therefore works through intelligent agents. These agents are manifold in kind.

The whole Cosmos is guided, controlled and animated by an almost endless series of Hierarchies or sentient Beings, each having a mission to perform, and who—whether we call them Dhyan Chohans or Angels—are 'Messengers' in the sense only that they are the agents of Cosmic or Karmic Laws. They vary infinitely in their respective degrees of consciousness and intelligence. . . . Each of these Beings was, or prepares to become, a man.[2]

Such are the Buddhist Avalokiteshvara and Amitabha, and the four 'Regents of the Earth' who appear in many mythologies, and the 'Thrones, Dominions and Powers' of Christianity. But there is an ancient tradition that by reason of their own past Karma certain human beings act

[1] Ibid.   [2] Ibid.

in a given life as focal points for mighty happenings, lightning conductors, as it were, through whom the Karmic force is 'earthed'. These are men to whom and about whom things of wide importance are always happening, whether they be at the head of a nation or a factory, but they are quite unconscious of their special, self-attracted function. Only a genuine Adept, one who has attained Enlightenment, can consciously control the forces of mass Karma, and so be a conscious agent of the Law. Incidentally, somewhere in this esoteric aspect of Karma must be incorporated the 'archetypal images' of Jung's discovery, but this, although a fruitful field for later research and consideration, is beyond the scope of the present volume.

Karmic Responsibilities

It would seem that man is responsible only for such acts as are generated in the mind. He is not, in other words, responsible for actions where the thought or intent did not run with the deed. If, for example, in turning quickly on a station platform someone bumps into a person standing close behind him, and so tips him on to the line in front of a train, he would not be responsible for a death which he never intended. Here the Law would seem to be the 'above' of which our English law is the reflected, though unconsciously reflected 'below'. For in English law there must, to constitute responsibility, not only be an *actus reus*, the wrongful deed, but also a *mens rea*, the wicked mind. A man is not responsible for a pure accident unless it was caused by such gross negligence that he must be held to have intended the 'natural and probable consequences' of his act. In the same way lunatics, children and persons completely drunk may be incapable of the *mens rea* which is a necessary ingredient of their responsibility.

This, however, is an over-simplification of an intensely difficult subject, for the latest discoveries in psychology enormously widen the range of the word 'intend'. One may, for example, 'intend' those acts which seem the very reverse of those apparently intended, and the most fantastic 'accident' may be a deliberate act by the unconscious, though fiercely repudiated by the conscious mind. Many an apparently accidental death, for example, is unconscious suicide, and many an injury caused to another may be deliberate at unconscious levels though unintended by the normal consciousness. The mind of man is a realm of which but a tithe is yet explored, and that but superficially, and the oft-repeated cry from the dock, 'I don't know what came over me', displays, to the trained psychologist, a hidden motive which the victim of his own unconscious genuinely denies.

One clue to the mystery may lie in the fact that an act has separate and often different effects on the various planes of consciousness. A millionaire, for example, may build a local hospital at vast expense and offer it to the town. The effect of his generosity will appear on different levels of his being. The outward deed was good, and will produce 'good' Karma, whatever the motive, but the mental effect will vary with the motive. If the reason of the gift was a genuine desire to use his worldly means for the benefit of his fellow men, his mind will be ennobled with the deed. If, on the other hand, his secret motive was the love of applause or, worse, a desire to curry local favour before standing as the town's representative in Parliament, then the effect on his mind will be that of the misuse of a power for selfish ends. This crude illustration will also explain the difference, so much insisted on in the famous *Sutra of Wei Lang*, between 'merits' and 'felicities'.

Such deeds [the Patriarch pointed out] as building temples, giving alms and entertaining the (Buddhist) Order will bring you only felicities, which should not be taken for merits. Merits are to be found within the Dharmakaya (Body of the Law), and have nothing to do with practices for attaining felicities.

Felicities, in other words, are pleasant Karma on the physical plane, but do not necessarily conduce to the attainment of Enlightenment. Merits, on the other hand, are reactions on the mind of mental welldoing or right motive, and are conducive to the mind's enlightenment.

Further light on our responsibility for 'accidents' is furnished by returning once again to the basic principles on which the Universe is built. Life is One, and all its forms are interrelated in a vastly complicated but inseverable whole. It follows that every act by any form of life, from the highest to the lowest, must react on every other form. The power of thought is terrifying, for thoughts are truly things, and once created have an independent existence of their own. The length and strength of this life depends on the intensity and clarity of the thinker's mind, but good or bad, each thought is a power, a living power for good or evil respectively. As such it affects not only the thinker, ennobling or debasing his mind for future thinking, but it affects all other life in the Universe. As A. P. Sinnet wrote in *The Occult World*:

Man is continually peopling his current in space with a world of his own, crowded with the offspring of his fancies, desires, impulses and passions; a current which reacts on any sensitive or nervous organization which comes in contact with it, in proportion to its dynamic intensity.

As the average mind is too undeveloped to confine the springs of action to its own thought alone, most men are at the mercy of the myriad thoughts which press upon the brain as bodies press one's body in a swaying crowd, and each man's actions are to that extent the effect not merely of his own volition but of the mass volition of the crowd. Hence the well-known phenomena of 'mob psychology', the power of slogans, the whims of fashion, the speed of rumour and, generally, the suggestibility of the weaker by the stronger mind.

Motive, therefore, is the dominating factor in every

act, for the act that springs from 'accident', if such there be, will at any rate have less effect than the carefully intended act. Acting from the highest levels in his being, man is the creative and controlling force in the Universe; acting from the lowest he is the worst enemy both of himself and the One Life. He can, if he did but know it, control the forces of nature consciously as he at present uses them unconsciously to produce their inevitable effect. Whether the user of these forces is 'white magic' or 'black magic' depends on the motive alone. Every act is in accordance with or against the stream of progress. He who swims with the current will the sooner reach the sea; he who swims against it will sooner or later suffer for his determined folly and in the end, broken and exhausted, move unwillingly down to the self-same sea.

Hour by hour we are choosing our direction, and the Law with utter justice acts accordingly. The choice between right and wrong is difficult enough to make at times, but the choice is harder still when it lies between right and right. Each man has many duties and many loyalties, and when they conflict it is hard to decide which is the more 'right' of the two. Yet the choice must be made, on principle and, if the heart be stout enough, 'in the scorn of consequence'. Thereafter the effect on various planes will mirror the wisdom and the selflessness of the decision made. Better, the Wisdom seems to say, a firm decision which, when found to be wrong, is as firmly changed and the punishment of error cheerfully borne than a vacillation which, if it breeds not error, breeds no right, and carries the weakling mind no further on the road to self-enlightenment.

Man as Karma

'Life becomes what it does.' There, in five words, is the essence of the Law. It follows that 'human history, from one point of view is nothing but a record of the Karma of Humanity, working itself out according to the good or evil of our racial, national and personal deeds'.[1]
Man *is* his Karma, and his deeds are part of him. Hence Maeterlinck's famous saying, 'Let us always remember that nothing befalls us that is not of the nature of ourselves.' Or, to quote from Edwin Arnold's *Light of Asia*,

> Karma—all that total of a soul
> Which is the things it did, the thoughts it had,
> The 'Self' it wove—with woof of viewless time
> Crossed on the warp invisible of acts— . . .

Compounded of good and evil, man as we know him is good in proportion as he has found the Light within, and learnt to 'let the Light shine'; and he is bad to the extent that he is still under the dominance of Maya, illusion, and lets himself be led by the lower, personal desire.

> Trishna, that thirst which makes the living drink
> Deeper and deeper of the false salt waves
> Whereon they float, pleasures, ambition, wealth,

[1] *Mysticism of East and West*, Loftus Hare.

Praise, fame or domination, conquest, love;
Rich meats and robes, and fair abodes and pride
Of ancient lines, and lust of days, and strife
To live, and sins that flow from strife, some sweet,
Some bitter . . .

Yet once again it must be emphasized that the soul,
wherein the ceaseless warfare between light and darkness,
right and wrong, is waged, is not immortal nor eternal;
still less is it changeless, for it is changing as a handful of
a river changes, with every new thought and act that
leaves or enters the whirlpool of the soul.

A Buddhist [wrote Mr R. J. Jackson[1]] will regard his property
as property, but not as his; will regard his body as body, but
not as his; will regard his sensations and ideas as sensations
and ideas, but not as his. . . . There is no truth in the thought
that 'this is mine and I have all these things'. If there is anything a man can truly call his own it is not what he possesses
but what he does.

The soul or Self is a ray of the SELF, and the mind that
decides its acts and motives is but a child of the Essence of
Mind, which is 'intrinsically pure'.

Rewards and Punishments

Man is punished by his sins, not for them. Karma
neither rewards nor punishes; it only restores lost harmony.
He who suffers deserves his suffering, and he who has
reason to rejoice is reaping where he has sown. But even

[1] *Buddhism and God.*

38

if all deserve their suffering, in that they have caused it, there is no excuse for callous indifference to their suffering by those more 'fortunate'. In the long run there is no such thing as personal Karma, for the acts of one are the acts of the whole, and the acts of the whole react on its littlest part. This vast and comprehensive blending of innumerable Karmas is the basis and the bedrock of the cosmic truth of Brotherhood. All things are in their essence good, and suffering is the servant of this Good. By that we learn, and in our common suffering move, by infinitely slow degrees, to that 'far off divine event to which the whole creation moves'.

The Doctrine of Merit

Nevertheless, though men are in essence One they are, at their present distance from enlightenment, separate entities, and though Karma reflects in all the acts of each, yet the average man is a Karmic unit, as it were, who suffers the good and evil results of his own actions. This fact is the basis of the doctrine of merit, of which so much appears in Buddhist literature. All good acts acquire merit for the actor in that at some future date, in this life or a later one, the cause will bear its due effect. This is a fact, but it is a low, unworthy motive for the doing of good deeds. As the Chinese Taoist, Chuang-Tzu, proclaimed, 'Rewards and punishments are the lowest form of education.' The reason is that behind such motive is the spur either of fear or else of low desire for the pleasure which the noble deed is believed to bring. This limitation of thought may serve, like blinkers, to keep the thinker to a simple ethical code, but will not produce enlightenment. In a talk to an American audience Krishnamurti said that such 'thought cannot escape from its limited action and reaction until it understands deeply and fully the cause and process of its own bondage'. When such limited thought expresses itself in action, he goes on, that action creates further limitation of thought.

Into this simple reality, reward and punishment have been introduced to deter so-called wrong action. If one is good—the good depending on limitation of thought, not upon understanding—then in the future or in the next life one will be suitably rewarded, and if one is not, one will be suitably punished. This element of fear, as reward and punishment, destroys understanding and love. If thought is influenced by reward and punishment, gain and loss, it cannot understand the craving that seeks reward and avoids punishment. Thought can only understand its own process if it does not identify itself with and cling to any of its own creations, any of its outgoing desires.

None the less, the doctrine of merit is a useful application of the Law of Karma to the daily round, for whatever the motive the habit of good deeds will purify the mind, and prepare it for greater widening of its scope. A better motive for right living is a wider appreciation of the Law and its relation to the Universe as a whole. With an understanding, however dim, of the basic unity of life

and the interrelation of all its members comes the desire
to assist all life towards enlightenment. This, refined still
further, awakens finally the highest springs of action, 'to
live by Law, acting the Law we live by without fear'; so
to have found and known the Essence of Mind that
nought is felt to be right save that which serves it utterly.
So long as merit and demerit is the motive-power of
action there is the danger of that heartless snobbery of
thought which, seeing suffering, remarks that it must be
the sufferer's Karma to suffer, and anyhow, what is it to
do with me? Such thought will bear its own result, a
further hardening of the heart which, blinded with its
dear delusion, continues to feel separate from its fellow
men and, like the Levite, passes by on the other side. Only
the light of compassion, an understanding love for all that
lives, can see that Karma as Law is a loving Law; that if it
is just it is also utterly merciful. We who on earth make
laws with which to judge our fellow men know that our
justice is fallible, and therefore add to the cold machinery
of justice the warmer quality of mercy which, so far
from dropping like a gentle dew from heaven, is a
virtue latent in the human heart. For 'Compassion is no
attribute. It is the Law of Laws,—eternal Harmony,
Alaya's. SELF; a shoreless universal essence, the light of
everlasting right, and fitness of all things, the law of Love
eternal'.[1] Only he who sees that law and justice and
mercy and love are so many aspects of the Law of

[1] *The Voice of the Silence.*

41

Harmony will understand that Karma is only a name we give that Law.

Classifications of Karma

The field of manifestation is subject to the illusion of time, for though in Reality all is Eternal Now, yet time is real to our senses. To our eyes there is past, present and future, and a cause and its effect are separated by an interval of time. In essence the cause-effect are as the two sides of a coin, inseverable and instantaneous, but we see them severally. It follows that we can, for purposes of understanding, analyse and classify the cause-effects of Karma, and four such classifications may be mentioned here.

Karma is often analysed in terms of time.

Karma [wrote W. Q. Judge in his *Aphorisms on Karma*] may be of three sorts: (*a*) Presently operative in this life through the appropriate instruments; (*b*) that which is being made or stored up to be exhausted in the future; (*c*) Karma held over from past life or lives, and not yet operating because inhibited by inappropriateness of the instrument in use by the Ego, or by the force of Karma now operating.

In the same way the twelve Nidanas, already described, are often grouped in three, ignorance and 'mental formations' belonging to the past lives, the next eight in the list to this life, and the last two, rebirth and decrepitude and death, belonging to the future life or lives. But whether 'Now working', 'In the making' or 'Held over', the

42

process is in fact indivisible. In terms of time, however, it is obvious that the complex causes of a busy life cannot all be worked out in that or in the succeeding life, and in any one life a man receives the results of only a small proportion of his own past causes, whether 'good' or 'bad'.

Karma reacts, as already explained, on all three planes, the mental, whence it originally sprang, the psychic and the physical, and the make-up of a man in any life will accord with the differing Karma that he has produced on the several planes of consciousness. A great mind may abuse its body and be reborn with a poorer one; a glorious body, exquisitely cared for, may harbour a poorly developed or even vicious mind. Yet the interaction is close. 'As we think, so we are', and evil thought will mar the body even as it shows in the face. Again, the evil in the mind may be rectified by a greater understanding long before the effect, say, of cruelty practised by the body has worked itself out on the physical plane. Hence the hunchback with a lovely mind.

In the well-known chapter on Karma in her *Buddhism, its Doctrines and Methods*, Madame David-Neel describes the Tibetan classification. General Karma perpetuates the round of existence as set out in the twelve Nidanas, which may be applied to all manifestation. Then comes Inanimate and Animate Karma. The Karma of 'inanimate' objects proceeds on the cyclic law of birth, growth, decay and death. Animate beings are subject in addition to moral Karma, that is, Karma that originates in the mind and for which the 'individual' is responsible. Finally, with man there is the still more particular Karma wherein he *is* his Karma, and as such and only as such moves from birth to birth towards enlightenment.

Finally, for the present purposes, Karma may be classified in terms of the size of the unit involved. A group or club or society may have its collective Karma as much as that smaller 'group of qualities' we call a man. In the same way a nation will not only reap the benefits and evil of its collective acts, but re-incarnate in the larger cycle of its destiny. Rome and Greece were units of rebirth, and the Punic wars are with us again to-day. Red Indians will appear in the race that slew them in such quantity, and many a minority movement in a country represents some olden enemy returned, this time, within the gates to continue an age-long war. He who would understand the pattern of history cannot ignore the doctrine of Karma; still less can he ignore Rebirth.

Summary

Karma, then, is the fundamental Law that rules all manifested things, and man, the conscious user of it, is but another aspect of the Namelessness. The Law was born when man was born, and will die 'when every blade of grass has entered into enlightenment'. It is utterly impersonal and absolutely just. It strives for harmony, and he who disturbs the harmony must suffer the adjust-

Summary

ment. The Law has agents, human and 'divine', yet these, the demi-gods, are likewise subject to its sway. Man is punished by his sins, not for them; it follows that there is no such thing as forgiveness and therefore none who can forgive. Yet the Law is merciful, for the Law is Love.

III

What Karma is not

Karma is not new. It is not a new theory of life to be idly discussed by the dilettante mind. Either it is a fundamental Law of the Universe or it is untrue.

It is not an Eastern doctrine, a product of an Eastern mode of thought. If it is true, it embraces not only East and West but the whole Universe, and the lightest study of Western literature for the last three thousand years will show that it has been held as true by most of the greatest minds.

Karma not anti-Christian

It is not opposed to Christianity, nor even incompatible with it. The principal differences between Christianity and Buddhism are in the nature and power of God and the nature of the 'soul'. The Buddhists say that God is so great that not only is this ultimate Principle absolutely impersonal, but it is 'beyond the range and reach of thought' and therefore even unnameable. 'THAT', as the Hindus call it, has no say in the affairs of any of its myriad parts, for all are parts or aspects of one inseverable Whole. To this extent and to this only Buddhists are atheists, in that they refuse to demean the ultimate Namelessness to the status of a tribal deity. On the question of soul the difference is subtle yet profound. The Christian believes that his soul, being 'divine', is immortal, and will go, when purged of sin, to heaven. The Buddhist proves, by sound analysis, that the soul or character, the ray of the One or spark of God or however it be described, so far from being immortal is changing every second of time (*anicca*), is lacking in any permanently separate or special factor which makes it different from any other aspect of the parent One (*anatta*), and being a (temporarily) separated part of the Whole, a child of illusion wandering in a world of Maya, is and will be the subject of suffering (*dukkha*), until that day when once again the 'dewdrop slips into the Shining Sea'. In other words, the Christian holds the soul to be the immortal part of man; the Buddhist presses the analysis of our being a whole stage further back and claims that nothing in man is eternal, but only that Oneness, the Essence of Pure Mind which, though it shines in every man, is never *his*. The light in an electric bulb shines through the bulb, but the bulb does not own it. Nor can it claim any 'piece' of electricity as being in its possession, for that which shines now in a billionth of a second is gone. There is but a river of life or light that flows through a myriad conduit pipes. None owns the river of Life, and he who holds its waters in his hand will find that in his attempt to possess the water he has stayed the flow, and all that he holds is 'dead'.

47

What Karma is not

It is, however, as difficult to speak of the teachings of Christianity, as if they were all agreed, as of the teachings of Buddhism. The Founders came, and taught, and went away. Their followers treasured all that they remembered of what they had, or thought they had, understood. This was later written down, or some of it, and thereafter generations of monkish editors added, subtracted and altered the script to accord with their own by no means settled views. Finally we have translations, as accurate as the understanding of the translator and no more. Such is the history of the Buddhist and Hindu Scriptures, and assuming that Jesus was an historic figure, such was the Christian tragedy too. It is said that there are three hundred sects of Chritianity; there are certainly six in Buddhism. But taking a reasonable consensus of belief in the two great religions, the differing views on 'soul' are of great importance. If I have a soul or, to be more accurate, *am* a soul with a body, and that soul is immortal and specially created by God at my birth, then I shall inevitably fight for the benefit and salvation of that soul, while vaguely hoping that those of my fellow men will be equally fortunate. The feeling is that of separation, save for the common Fatherhood of a God whose ways are unpredictable. If, on the other hand, I know that nothing of the SELF is mine, that all of me is *anicca*, *anatta* and a prey to *dukkha*, then selfishness and personal ambition have no purpose and are seen as foolishness; and though in the fight against the illusion of selfish purposing I may and shall be vanquished again and again, still, at least I know that 'there is no abiding Self in man', and that every single form of life, and there is nothing 'dead', is equally Divine.

So much for differences. But are they ancient or modern? St Paul unquestionably taught the doctrine of Karma and Rebirth, and many of Christ's sayings are meaningless unless they refer to a doctrine so well known to his audience. But more of this hereafter. At the moment it is enough to observe that Karma is not by any means anti-Christian.

Karma not Good or Bad

Karma is neither good nor bad, and it is inaccurate to speak of 'good Karma' and 'bad Karma'. Karma *is*; how we view it is our own affair. None but an adept, a Master of the Law, can judge another's Karma. We who see but a few strands of the web cannot know the design of which these tangled threads are part. What may seem at the time misfortune may, by clearing away the refuse of past error, open a way to further advancement; good fortune may so puff up the recipient that from spiritual pride he falls to the ground again, and suffering tests and strengthens character. The habit of avoiding man-made labels for the day's events is itself an advance in character. It is a sign of strength to appreciate that everything that is has had a cause, and that all that befalls one is genuinely 'right'. As Epictetus said, 'True instruction is this: to learn to wish that each thing should come to pass as it does. And how does it come to pass? As the Disposer has disposed it.' For Epictetus the Disposer was no personal God but a natural Principle, which in its operation is the Law of Karma. Man-made labels do not clarify; they cloud the mind to proper values. As is written in a Japanese Scripture,

Since everything in this world is caused by the concurrence of causes and conditions, there can be no fundamental distinction between things. The apparent distinctions exist because of people's absurd and deluding thoughts and desires. In the sky there is no distinction of East and West; people create the distinction out of their own minds and then believe it to be true.

The anonymous writer of this ancient Scripture goes much further, and his words accord with the parent Indian philosophy.

In the universal process of becoming there are inherently no distinctions between the process of life and the process of destruction; people make a distinction and call the one birth and the other death. In action there is no distinction between right and wrong, but people make a distinction for their own silly convenience. . . . To Buddha every definite thing is illusion, something which the mind constructs; he knows that whatever the mind can grasp and throw away is vanity; thus he avoids the pitfalls of images and discriminative thought.

Predestination and Freewill

Once the Law of Karma is understood it will be seen that there is no such thing as luck, good or bad, but, to quote from the Stoic Emperor, Marcus Aurelius, 'Subsequents follow antecedents by a bond of inner consequence; it is no merely numerical sequence of arbitrary and isolated units, but a rational interconnection.' Nor is the doctrine of Karma equivalent to the doctrine of Predestination or Determinism. Still less is it Fatalism. 'The latter implies a blind course of some still blinder power, but man is a free agent during his stay on earth',[1] free, that is, within the working of the Law. For, viewed from one life, the 'operative' Karma of that life is equivalent to the Greek Nemesis or Destiny. But this destiny is not the decree of a wrathful God but the product of that man's imagining. 'The fault, dear Brutus, is not in our stars but in ourselves that we are underlings.' In order, however, to understand Professor Radhakrishnan's dictum, 'Freedom and Karma are two aspects of the same reality', it may be wise to return to first principles.

The soul of man, as distinct from 'his' spirit and the physical body, is the battleground of the 'pairs of oposites' which, ranged under the banners of Good and Evil, contend for the mastery. On the side of light is the will, in the sense of the driving force towards enlightenment; on the other are the massed desires of the lower, personal self which craves for its separative own aggrandizement. These two forces strive unceasingly, and now the one and now the other gains the field. Such is

[1] *The Secret Doctrine*, H. P. Blavatsky.

'the sickness of the spirit (soul)' [as St Augustine called it] 'that raiseth itself not to its full stature, being sustained by the truth but weighed down by custom. And thus there are two wills, and neither is entire. . . .'

Bearing in mind this internal duality of the soul, and remembering that the mind is the father of Karma and that it is choosing every moment whether its acts shall be 'good' or 'bad', the words of the writer Pascal will provide the solution to the problem of Freewill and Destiny, which is in fact no problem at all. 'Though slaves of the past,' he wrote, 'we are masters of the future.' The following analogy may help. A man is in a room with two doors. He piles up the furniture against one door and falls asleep. Later he wakes, and complains that he has no choice of exit, for there is only one door available. The answer is—remove the furniture. It sometimes happens that a man may truly say, 'There seemed no other course open to me—I had no choice.' But it is he who by his own past action piled up the furniture against the alternate door. He is bound by his fate, but he *is* his fate, and nothing in the world save his own debility of will prevents him becoming free. There are many who cry in the bonds of circumstance, 'I bow before the will of God.' But as there is no God save the God within, whose instrument is Karma, we have but one excuse for our bondage, that we lack the will to be free.

If there is no luck or chance there is no such thing as coincidence. However amazing the said 'coincidence', each set of facts was the result of previous causes. But whether the additional fact that the results fell out so strangely to our eyes has any significance is a different matter, for Law is Law but meaning is what we add to it, and the meaning drawn from any facts will vary with the individual. Many apparent coincidences are clearly the effects of previous acts. The innumerable stories of people who, by an amazing series of events, are drawn to a particular place or away from it at the moment when a terrible event takes place are not in the least 'accidents'. For some reason, which nought but a Master could trace, that person was 'meant', or was not 'meant', to be killed when the bomb fell, or whatever the event might be. Taking the matter on a larger scale, it may be that a man who is incarnated into a particular family or race at a particular time was guided there by his Karma, under the laws of affinity, in order that he might be subject to the working out of national Karma, whether of war or earthquake or a period of prosperity. In a work of this size, however, it is impossible to speculate on the working out of the Law. It is enough to explain what seem to be its basic principles, and leave the individual, with an awakening intuition, to study for himself the Law which in a sense he is.

IV

What Karma explains

Once the Law is reasonably understood it solves a large proportion of the problems which cloud our present mind, and certainly in the East, where Karma is as obvious as the law of gravity, these problems do not arise.

In the first place it explains the inequities and inequalities of daily life. Only Karma

can explain the mysterious problem of Good and Evil, and reconcile man to the terrible *apparent* injustice of life. For when one unacquainted with the noble doctrine looks around him, and observes the inequalities of birth and fortune, of intellect and capacities; when one sees honour paid to fools and profligates, and their nearest neighbour, with all his intellect and noble virtues, perishing of want and for lack of sympathy; when one sees all this and has to turn away, helpless to relieve the undeserved suffering, that blessed knowledge of Karma alone prevents him from cursing life and men, as well as their supposed Creator.[1]

On the other hand, nothing is more untrue than the cry that all men are born equal. They are not. Each is born with the burden, pleasant or unpleasant, of his own

[1] *The Secret Doctrine*, H. P. Blavatsky.

Karma, and no two men are equal, for no two are the same.

All mankind is one family, but its members are of different ages. Therefore there is no equality of opportunity and no equality of responsibility. Although all are marching towards a common goal they cannot bear equal burdens, and would not be expected to if the Law of Karma were understood.[1]

In the same way Karma explains the problem of Original Sin. There is no problem, for there is no original sin. First causes are necessarily unknowable, and as the Buddha insisted again and again, discussion of such matters is unprofitable, as leading in no way to the heart's enlightenment. But the teaching of the Wisdom is clear. Evil is man-made, and is of his choosing, and he who suffers suffers from his deliberate use of his own free will. Cripples, dwarfs and those born deaf or blind are the products of their own past actions, and one's pity should be used, not in bewailing the injustice of their condition, but in assisting the new-born brain to appreciate its own responsibility and to produce new causes whose result will be the undoing of the evil whose results are manifest. Infant prodigies, on the other hand, are clearly the result of specialization in some particular line, and even special aptitudes and preferences are the outcome of the Law.

Conscience is a Karmic memory. The Essence of Mind

[1] *The Scales of Karma*, Owen Rutter.

is deathless, and its ray, the consciousness (*vinnana*) which moves from life to life, is a store-house of immensely complex memory. Even though the brain, which is new in each life, has forgotten the lessons of past experience, the inner mind remembers, and when temptation murmurs again of the pleasures of a certain low desire, the voice of memory replies, 'But what of the cost in suffering, the price that you paid?'

Heredity versus Environment

Karma explains. ' "Karma", expresses, not that which a man inherits from his ancestors, but that which he inherits from himself in some previous state of existence.'[1] In the same way, environment is a product of one's own past actions, for each new birth accords with the Karma therein to be discharged. All that is inherited from parents is the body, the outermost garment of the many-robed, essential man. The mind, or returning unit of consciousness, so far from being the product of its body's parents, chose those parents, and the body which they would provide for the working out of a portion of past Karma. Heredity is therefore the servant of Karma and not its substitute. By the law of affinity, the magnetic law of attraction and repulsion, each new body attracts an appropriate 'soul' or character, as each returning consciousness attracts or is attracted to a vehicle suitable for self-expression in the life to come. The staggering com-

[1] *Buddhism in Translations*, Henry Clarke Warren.

plexity of such elaborate choosing, allowing for period, race, sex, family and the compound circumstances of 'environment', is a reason for the mind's humility before the Law, but no bar to its acceptance. If an automatic telephone exchange can be made to 'choose' which of a dozen lines is the least 'loaded' at the moment, how much more can the Namelessness in manifestation operate its own high purposes!

Karmic Cycles

Modern astronomy has reached considerable knowledge of the stellar cycles, and even modern astrology, the half-understood remains of a once esoteric and spiritual science, has much to say on planetary cycles and their effect on man. Indian philosophy has a complete record of 'Yugas', great and small, covering enormous periods of time, and of cycles, wheels within wheels, as regular as the ebb and flow of the tide. These cycles affect all planes of manifestation, the psychic and mental as well as the physical, but the law which governs these cycles cannot be understood save in the context of the wider, Karmic Law. The obvious example of the working of the Law on a mass unit of humanity is the rise and fall of races or sub-races, which may or may not be coincident with nations. Whole civilizations are known to have risen, flourished, reached a great height of culture and then decayed or, as in the case of the Khmers of Indo-China, suddenly disappeared. Modern Greece, though still, as the world now knows, a magnificent fighting nation, is not to be compared in culture with its classic forebear; Spain and Portugal are not what they were; Mexico has sunk to comparative insignificance. On the other hand, many a nation now at its prime has risen suddenly, and in the round of time will as surely fall. Ethnologists are always puzzled at the causes of a tribe's collapse and disappearance, and only an understanding of the Law of Karma-Rebirth will solve the mystery. It is not that a given tribe or race by hereditary evolution of its inherent abilities grows rapidly from mediocrity to genius, but that an ever higher standard of 'souls' find in the rising race opportunity for their own development. In due course, when the cycle has reached its greatest height, these great ones, far on the road of genius in their several ways, begin to leave, and with the assistance of external causes, themselves Karmic, such as disease, sterility, conquest or moral decay, the race dies out.

The Cause of War

One of the obvious cycles is that of peace and war. War is an effect, the mass-effect of mass thinking, and once the cause is produced the effect is inevitable. The cause of war, as of all evil, is the 'Three Fires' burning in the human mind, desire, hatred and illusion. Hatred is born of illusion, the illusion that life is separate, the ignorance of man's essential unity, and desire, or its negative aspect, fear, is the product of and in turn engenders hate.

The Cause of War

Were no man to hurt his brother, Karma-Nemesis would have neither cause to work for, nor weapons to act through. It is the constant presence in our midst of every element of strife and opposition, and the division of races, nations, tribes, societies and individuals into Cains and Abels, wolves and lambs, that is the chief cause of the 'ways of Providence.' [1]

Hate is a force, a tremendous force, and mass hate slowly accumulates as a thunder-cloud in the sky. When the opposing thought-forms on the psychic plane have reached a point of over-loading it needs but the lightning flash to cause a discharge. But the analogy is insufficient. When the thunder-cloud has fallen the tension is over; the discharge itself does not, in the ordinary sense, produce another cloud. But in war there is hate, deliberate cruelty, revenge and lust. All these are causes, and each must bear its inevitable effect. Thus wars are the cause of wars, and a 'war to end war' is one of the wilder illusions of the human mind.

Even in peace we are causing war.

In our daily life we are competitive, aggressive, nationalistic, vengeful and self-seeking, which inevitably culminates in war. Intellectually and emotionally we are influenced and limited by the past, which produces the present reaction of hate, antagonism and conflict. . . . Until our own lives are no longer aggressive and greedy, and psychologically we cease from seeking security, and so breaking up the world into

[1] *The Secret Doctrine*, H. P. Blavatsky.

different classes, races, nationalities and religions, there cannot be peace.[1]

The cause of war, therefore, is the individual mind which, in its ignorance of man's essential unity, wants everything for itself and therefore hates and fears its fellow men. But this war is an everlasting war within, and until each human being has slain the foe within he will not find peace without. 'The man who wars against himself and wins the battle can do it only when he knows that in that war he is doing the one thing which is worth doing.'[2]

Foretelling the Future

If the future is the past and present not yet come, then it should be as possible to predict the future as it is to predict the future weather, providing, and it is a very large proviso, that all the causal factors are known. But just as a meteorologist can only predict from his known facts, and there are usually factors of which he has no information, so the fortune-teller, whether he be an astrologer dealing in world astrology or some other type considering the affairs of an individual, can only calculate from known factors to the resultant effect which is not yet manifest. If a single factor is missing the whole calculation is worthless. Much 'fortune-telling', however, is the work of persons whose psychic faculties,

[1] *Krishnamurti. Notes of a Talk in America.*
[2] *Practical Occultism*, H. P. Blavatsky.

though quite untrained, are more awake than is usual in
the Western world. They 'feel', by means of cards or
other devices for concentrating their faculties, the cloud
of unexpected Karma in the aura, or psychic envelope,
and try to read it. Being untrained they are seldom accurate,
and though palmistry, physiognomy and the like might
conceivably, at a later stage in man's evolution, develop
into sciences, they are, at our present stage, a poor substitute for knowledge, even assuming that such knowledge
is to be desired. But is it? Or does this morbid craving to
lift the veil of the future lead but to a weakening of the
will? Certainly it is a miserable substitute for the planned
and purposeful development of all one's faculties by the
conscious user of the Law. The first type wonders what
the future will bring; the other decides it.

Further Advantages

The advantages of working by the Law of Karma have
no end. As already explained, the Law provides a
graded sanction or reason for right living. At the worst,
it is seen that it pays to be good; higher than this, it proves
that men are in essence one, and that any deed which hurts
one's neighbour or the commonweal is an injury to oneself; finally, it reveals a world or a plane of consciousness
where right becomes the inmost law of being, and a man
does right, not because it pays or because it avoids self-
injury, but because, beyond all argument, he must.

Karma destroys the cause of envy and jealousy and the

consequent ill-will, for your neighbour is more fortunate than you because he has earned a better fortune. It removes impatience, for when there is all but infinite time ahead, why worry the fretful hour? It largely removes the fear of death, for where there is inner conviction of rebirth and, by the law of affinity, reunion sooner or later with those one loves, why worry that the hour must come for leaving the present robes and resting, ere returning, robed anew, for fresh experience?

Karma and Modern Psychology

Psychology, the Cinderella of Western science, is yet in its infancy, but any doctrine must sooner or later come to terms with it. Here is a fascinating field for research and experiment. Industrial psychologists, for example, are troubled with the problem of the 'accident prone' workmen who are always suffering or somehow being mixed up in unnecessary 'accidents'. An American scientist writes that 'it has been completely proved, beyond all shadow of doubt, that the elimination of certain men from industrial plants met with a decrease if not a cessation of accidents in that plant'. From the personal point of view these men may have 'unconsciously-deliberately' caused the accidents; from the mass point of view they may be Karmic agents, that is, as W. Q. Judge defined it, 'one who concentrates more rapidly than usual the lines of influence that bring about events, sometimes in a strange and subtle way'.

Karma and Psychology

Karma would seem to be the missing link in modern psychology. Surely 'complexes' are only deposits in the unconscious from action and reaction in past lives, and 'character deficiencies', gaps in the moral development of the patient, defy the physician's skill because none can implant in another's mind a virtue which, though there potentially, has not been developed in the lives gone by. In other words, the psychologist, however skilful his analysis, can only restore the position at birth, removing the knots and inhibitions of wrong thinking and leaving the patient free to resume the path of development with less impediment and wasted energy. The application of psychology to crime, and in particular juvenile delinquency, would be far easier if the psychologist appreciated that he must look further back than the criminal's childhood for the true cause of the crime, and the whole field of insanity should be revised in the light of the Karmic Law. These, however, are the exceptions, for the West has need of applying the Law to the many, not only to the few. The outlook on life of the 'man in the street' could be utterly changed by a knowledge of Karma, and he who accepts it as a reasonable hypothesis will find by his own experience that the Law is true, and that he who uses it is master of life and death, and the sole custodian of his destiny.

V

Some Difficulties considered

Many persons on being first introduced to Karma demand the precise details of its working, and failing to receive them refuse to accept the Law. It is useful to ask them in reply if they know the nature of electricity. If they are truthful they answer, No. To which one may reply, Nor does one know the nature of Karma but, like our knowledge of electricity, we know just a little how it works. The rest is a matter of research and experience.

It is a strange aberration of the mind that refuses to accept a law of life because it cannot at present grasp its detailed working. We use X-rays, but know very little about them; use wireless and we are only on the fringe of 'how it works'; and though we have used the laws of light for three generations we are now discovering that our knowledge, at any rate of the straightness of its rays, was far from full. Karma is true or untrue, and only the individual can decide in which category to place it. But to refuse to accept it on the ground that our knowledge of its working is limited is, to say the least of it, an immodest point of view.

It is sometimes said that Karma is cold, that it is heartless. Karma is neither warm nor cold. It *is*. But those who are justly fearful of a world wherein law, as they conceive the term, is paramount, and love excluded from its scope, have nought to fear. If Karma is the Law of Harmony, so is love. Like Karma, 'Compassion is no mere attribute. It is the Law of LAWS, eternal Harmony.' So runs *The Voice of the Silence*, which is one of the oldest books in the world. Karma is an aspect of the One, the Unnameable; love is another. If Karma controls the relations of the myriad parts to each other and the Whole, love is the cement that binds them all in One. He who regards Karma as a Law and his brother as separate from himself does not understand Karma. There is but one Karma, though each part of the wholeness suffers the effects of what the smallest part has caused. My brother's suffering is my own and mine is his, and 'in my brother's face I see my own unanswered agony'. To say of a suffering friend, 'It is his Karma,' may be true, but to assume that therefore it is not yours too is to prison the heart in the iron bars of illusion, and it is the heart which so regards its neighbour, not the Law, that is cold.

Interfering with Karma

One cannot 'interfere' with Karma, as many seem to suppose. A man may have placed himself in a serious predicament, and a friend is fearful lest, in helping him, he is 'interfering' in the working out of his Karma. The friend fails to realize that it may be the man's Karma that he should be helped, and the help or withholding of it is just as much his Karma as his present suffering. The misconception probably arises from the Western preoccupation with its neighbour's affairs, for we are so bent on 'social service' that we forget a greater duty still, our own improvement. Yet the Biblical story of the mote and the beam should be borne in mind, and practised. There may be nothing finer than self-forgetfulness, but the very thought of whether or not one is interfering is self-remembrance, not forgetfulness, and he who helps wherever help is needed, and for the rest removes his own beams from his eye, is doing his duty, and no man can do more. The question has been raised in extreme form by certain pacifists who, refusing to lend themselves to violence, equally refuse to help a dying man in an air-raid lest they should seem to be taking part in the war. Egotism could hardly go further, and such absorption in selfish thinking is pathetic. The Law of compassion, which never clashes with that of Karma, overrides all else. 'Inaction in a deed of mercy becomes an action in a deadly sin.'[1] Karma will act according to its nature, and needs no help from any man. He who acts according to his heart, as controlled by experience and sweet reasonableness, may act in error, but only by error will he learn his error. For the rest he will earn the merit of doing what he feels to be right, and no man can do more.

[1] *The Voice of the Silence.*

Vicarious Atonement

Those who have studied the Buddhism of the Northern or Mahayana School will have read of the doctrine of merit, and of certain men or bodies of men being 'fields of merit' for the commonweal. It is obvious that a person with a lovely mind will shed a radiance round him in which all may share, and a monastery of persons leading a holy life will radiate its own vibration. But when it is suggested that their efforts will neutralize the 'evil' Karma of others the door is open to the dangerous doctrine of 'vicarious atonement'. The dangers are obvious. 'Work out your own salvation,' said the Buddha, and there would be chaos indeed if any Being, however great, could 'forgive' another's sins.

Each time that a repentant sinner is assured that the effects of causes he himself set in operation can be nullified by forgiveness from any source, he is being taught an untruth which cannot but imperil the future development of his soul. Each time a priest pronounces absolution over some terrified being whom the shadows of the gallows, perhaps, has frightened into 'repentance' after a long life of selfishness and crime, he assumes an authority and a power which is absolutely at variance with the law to which he owes his own existence.[1]

The doctrines of vicarious atonement and Karma are therefore incompatible. But the doctrine of vicarious salvation is a little different, and though easily abused, has

[1] *Reincarnation*, Anderson.

67

a foundation in one aspect of the Karmic Law. Remembering man's essential unity, both with other forms of life and with the Law which is another aspect of the Namelessness, it may be seen how the goodly deeds of one may benefit and so hasten, though never alone procure, the 'salvation' of another. The Bhikkhu Silacara has much to say on the subject in his pamphlet, *Kamma*. When, he says, a Buddhist performs an act of merit, and on the pagoda-platform, after offering incense and flowers before the image of the Buddha, strikes a great bell which lies beside him, he is not calling on the supposed keeper of the records of Kamma for another item to be put to the credit of that person.

What he is saying is this: 'All ye to whose ears comes the sound of this bell, know that a deed of merit has just been performed. The doer of the deed hereby gladly offers you a share of his merit from the doing of the good deed, and begs you with equal gladness to accept it.'

This is a very different thing from expecting the deeds of others to atone for one's own misdoing. To radiate love to all beings is one of the standard meditations of Buddhist practice, and its object, besides suffusing the heart of the meditator with unbounded love, is to assist all living things in their development. For the effect of love is to kill out hate, to dissolve the illusion of selfishness and to reduce the unworthy desire which is the cause of suffering. If every living thing experiences to some extent the acts of every other, then each can deliberately strive to see that the effects of his own causing are, so far as he can control them, good. Once more, therefore, the inseparability of the threads of Karma is a clue to a doctrine which, though easily and frequently abused, is spiritually true.

'Unmerited Suffering'

The same clue may provide the solution to another problem, that of 'unmerited suffering'. Do we deserve all that happenes to us, or are there occasional 'accidents' in which we suffer without justice? An immediate answer would be that if so, there must equally be unmerited happiness, for which in due course we must compensate with suffering, and that on balance the cosmic harmony, within and by the Law of Karma, would be restored. The key to the problem is time, one of the necessary illusions of manifestation. It would be impossible, at least to our conception, to guide an incoming 'soul' to a body and set of circumstances which exactly accord with its needs and deserts, and all that did not do so, pleasant or unpleasant, would presumably be the subject of later adjustment by the all-embracing and utterly just Law.

Karma and Duty

There are some who find difficulty in reconciling Karma and duty. If all that we do is what we are, and according as we are so we act, what, they ask, is the place of duty in the Law's machinery? The answer imports a new term, Dharma (in Pali, Dhamma), which, like most key-words in Oriental philosophy, is untranslatable.

Many words have been suggested in translation, among them Law, Duty, the Good, the True, Righteousness, the Norm, the Ideal and even the Way, but it is the symbol of a concept of too complex a nature to admit of translation by any one English term. . . . It may be described as the outward manifestation of a body of Teaching, Moral Law, Doctrine or system of philosophy which has existed for all time, in the abstract world of thought, which is Plato's 'Noumenal Realm'. Hence the meaning of Norm, or Ideal Form, as the clothing of a vast idea. . . .[1]

Considering the word as duty, that which in 'rightness' should be done, it has been said that the Dharma of one life is that portion of the individual's Karma due to be discharged or worked out in that life. As such, it is one's 'duty' to face it, accept it and so be rid of it, whether it be 'good' or 'evil'. Hence the insistence in nearly every occult work on the due performance of all duty, from the *Bhagavad Gita* and the Bible to *The Voice of the Silence* and the *Dhammapada*. To quote from the last, 'By oneself evil is done; by oneself one suffers. By oneself evil is left undone; by oneself one is purified. Purity and impurity belong to oneself; no one can purify another'—and then: 'Let no one forget his own duty for the sake of another's, however great; let a man, when he has discerned his own duty, be always attentive to it.' This does

[1] *What is Buddhism?* The Buddhist Lodge, London.

but echo the admonition of the *Bhagavada Gita*, that 'there is danger in another's duty', and this belief is the basis of the Eastern virtue of minding one's own business which the West, in its enthusiasm for social service and good works, is apt to ignore. In either part of the world, however, all pilgrims of the Path agree that 'the immediate work, whatever it may be, has the abstract claim of duty, and its relative importance and non-importance is not to be considered at all'. And again, 'There can be no permanent rest or happiness as long as there is some work to be done, and not accomplished, and the fulfilment of duties brings its own reward'.[1] He who is wise has faith in the Law, and knows that in doing what he believes to be right he is using the Law to the advantage of mankind.

[1] *Practical Occultism*, H. P. Blavatsky.

VI

Rebirth

Certain writers have distinguished shades of meaning between the doctrines of Metempsychosis, Transmigration, Pre-existence and Rebirth, but for present purposes the word Rebirth is used to cover the doctrine which, from the human point of view, is the inseparable twin of Karma. In this sense, just as physical progress is effected through hereditary transmission, so spiritual progress is achieved by the process of rebirth. Cause and effect are an indivisible unity, but in the illusion of time the one follows the other. In the opinion of the Bhikkhu Silacara,

One might even say that they are the same doctrine, looked at in one case subjectively, and in the other objectively. In a manner of speaking, Kamma is rebirth latent, and for the time being unmanifest; and rebirth is Kamma become active and manifest.

From another point of view, the lessons of Karma necessitate a school wherein they may be learnt; Rebirth provides such a school whose 'terms' and 'holidays' succeed one another until the final lesson is learnt.

The Reincarnating Entity

It has been seen that that which reincarnates is not an immortal soul but the product of countless previous lives, a bundle of attributes called Character which is changing from moment to moment, and lacks any element of immortality which it could truthfully claim as its own. On the other hand, each such returning unit of life is a ray or spark or aspect of the Wholeness which, through the slow experience of its myriad points of consciousness, collectively attains self-consciousness, or, in the words of the mystics, 'finds Itself'. The Brahmin philosophy speaks of Atman (Pali, Atta), the Spirit in man which is his share in the Absolute, as it were, but by the Buddha's time this spiritual conception had been debased, as in modern Christianity, to that of an immortal soul. Against this degradation of a mighty truth the Buddha taught the doctrine of An-atta—*not-* (immortal) Soul— destroying the wrong conception of the positive by stressing the negative. In the well-known story of Vaccha-gotta the Wanderer, there is a passage on the nature of self which explains the Buddhist and therefore the true Brahmin point of view. Vacchagotta asked the Buddha what he had to say about the Self, but the Blessed One refused to answer. When the questioner had departed in disgust, the Venerable Ananda enquired the reason for his silence. 'If I had answered that the Self exists,' the Buddha said, 'that would be to side with those who are eternalists.

73

But if, Ananda, I had replied that the Self does not exist, that would be to side with those who are annihilationists.' The answer is further elaborated, but the point is already clear. The Self is and is not. That which is reborn is the old man and yet a new. The soul is immortal, but it is changing every hour. As an immortal entity there is no soul, even, as a personal deity, there is no God.

Analogies sometimes help, and a favourite theme of Buddhist exegesis is the flame.

Life is a flame, and transmigration, new becoming, is the transmitting of the flame from one combustible aggregate to another; just that, and nothing more. If we light one candle from another, the communicated flame is one and the same, in the sense of an observed continuity, but the candle is not the same.[1]

Note that each candle perishes, but the flame lives on, and note that the flame, though in a way a particular flame, is in essence Light, and as such common to all.

The proximate force or energy which out of the past material produces a new 'being' is Trishna, the thirst for sentient existence, the libido of modern psychology, but Karma is the guiding power behind. The 'three fires' whose burning craves for further fuel are hatred, lust and illusion. Hate is a powerful force, and draws the hater into perpetual close relation with the person hated until he learns that 'hatred ceaseth not by hatred, hatred ceaseth but by love'; lust, or personal desire in every

[1] *Buddha and the Gospel of Buddhism*, Coomaraswamy.

form, is an obvious cause of life after life on the Wheel of Rebirth, but the strongest force is illusion, the Maya of ignorance about this very truth of Anatta. For 'the human mind discriminates itself from the things that appear to be outside itself without realizing that it has first created those very things within its own mind',[1] and one of the things which it has itself created is the separation between self and self. Hence the 'Great Heresy' of Attavada, belief in the separative self.

To sum up on this all-important matter of the nature of the thing reborn, there are three selves in man, or, more correctly, he functions at three main levels of consciousness. The mind

on its lowest level is a discriminating mind; on this level it has the ability to see, hear, taste, smell, touch, to combine these sense concepts, to discriminate them, and to consider their relations. On a higher level it is an intellectual mind, where it has the ability to make the inward adjustments that are necessary to harmonize the reactions of the discriminating mind and to relate them to each other and to a whole ego conception. On its highest level it is Universal Mind.[1]

These levels correspond exactly with the 'body, soul and spirit' of St. Paul, and it is at the middle level, that of the 'soul', that man, the potentially immortal Essence of Pure Mind, reincarnates unceasingly until the potential has become the actual and the 'dewdrop' has become the 'Shining Sea'.

[1] From a Japanese Scripture.

Rebirth

The New Body

The new life accords with the deserts, or part of them, of all preceding births. By the law of attraction the incoming man is drawn into the current which will land him in an environment most suited to his (spiritual) needs. Whether the new-born soul dislikes or likes its environment is immaterial. It made its bed, and now must lie on it. In the new life it may be following still further a line of development already begun; hence definite proclivities in one direction and the desire to pursue them; or it may strike out in a new, and possibly complementary line of progress; or it may, by reason of causes 'good' or 'bad' of past behaviour, find itself with utterly new environment and different opportunities for self-expression. In the words of the *Light of Asia*:

> Who toiled a slave may come anew a Prince
> For gentle worthiness and merit won;
> Who ruled a King may wander earth in rags
> For things done and undone.

But such a change is not necessarily for the worse. Christ reminded his followers that the rich man's lot was a spiritually hard one, for wealth is apt to bind the awakening mind, and he who clings to wealth of pocket or mind will lose it, even as only he who gives away his very life shall find it.

It will be noted that the mind chooses the body and is not its child, as is still the belief of Western materialism.

The Choice of Body

The soul chooses the body most suited to its needs, and therefore comes into the family which will provide that body. If a lawyer wishes further experience as a lawyer he will probably enter a legal family. If so, he will be a lawyer not because his father was a lawyer, but because, being already a lawyer, a 'legal' brain in the new body will make his task the easier. Other factors are the rhythm of the sexes, of the introvert and extrovert types of mind, and of a thousand other complementary types of character, while men may change the pattern of their lives as the years go by and with it the kind of experience they gain. In all there is infinite variety; not even the element of progress is constant, for blinded with illusion a man may in a single life undo the accumulated merit of many lives preceding, and every conquest made is painfully relative to the distance yet to be run.

> Veil after veil will lift—but there must be
> Veil upon veil behind.

Change of Values

Those who accept or re-accept the Law of Karma will find that the new conception radically alters the prevailing point of view. Parents, for example, are seen with new eyes; friends are probably old friends, and foes old enemies. Places and people and even things are 'remembered'. The body is seen as an instrument to be, as a dog or horse, well cared for but well disciplined. The various parts in the drama-comedy of life are seen for what they are, so

many masks assumed for the part, then laid aside when
the play is ended. The mental eyes are shortened and yet
lengthened in their view. On the one hand, now is the
time that matters, now when the lightest act is building
the days unborn, here where the effects of every act must
be digested, not in a heaven or hell to be known hereafter. On the other hand, death is not the end of the
adventure. Infinite time is ours for the using, and the
space available is commensurate with the Universe. And
the struggle is worth while.

> Yea! whoso, shaking off the yoke of flesh
> Lives Lord, not servant, of his lusts; set free
> From pride, from passion, from the sin of 'Self',
> Toucheth tranquillity! . . .
> Live where he will,
> Die when he may, such passeth from all 'plaining
> To blest Nirvana, with the Gods, attaining.

And Nirvana is but the death of 'self', the self that in its
piteous pride is unaware that it is of the Essence of Pure
Mind.

Yet sooner or later each incarnation comes to an end.
The mask begins to perish and the actor, laden with new
experience received through his senses and his perishable
brain, longs for a period of rest wherein to digest the
lessons of that life. And so the body dies, not of death
but of too much life. The pressure of the electric current
in time wears out the lamp, and the lamp must be re-

newed. Life never tires, nor ages; only the form grows old. At the body's death there is no occasion for grief, and if we mourn we mourn but for our foolish selves.

When the day's work is ended, night brings the benison of sleep. So death is the ending of a larger day, and in the night that follows every man finds rest, until of his own volition he returns to fresh endeavour and to labours new. So has it been with this our brother, so will it be for all of us, until the illusion of a separated self is finally transcended, and in the death of self we reach Enlightenment.[1]

When the body has been consumed with fire, and so as swiftly as possible reduced to its natural elements, it is best forgotten. The friend remains, and by a law beyond all breaking will be met with in the lives to come.

After Death

The period between lives can never be the subjec relatable experience, and anything said of it rests on a different footing from the principles and doctrines above set out, for these are not only the accumulated experience of mankind, but are capable of verification by all who study them. But the same immemorial Wisdom is as precise about the period between lives as it is clear in its condemnation of 'bhuta-worship', the intercourse with the astral remains of the dead which the West calls

[1] From a Buddhist Funeral Service.

Rebirth

spritualism. The purpose of this book being to make Karma and Rebirth a living reality in the mind of those who accept it, any discussion on post-mortem states of being is only of marginal interest, but for the sake of completeness reference may be made to Letter XXV of *The Mahama Letters to A. P. Sinnett*, where the subject, referred to casually in numerous works of Eastern wisdom, is usefully summed up.

There are two fields of causal manifestation, the objective and subjective. So the grosser energies, those which operate in the heavier or denser conditions of matter, manifest objectively in physical life, their outcome being the new personality of each birth included within the grand cycle of the evolving individuality. The moral and spiritual activities find their sphere of effects in 'devachan'.... Bacon, for instance, whom a poet called 'The greatest, wisest, *meanest* of mankind', might reappear in his next incarnation as a greedy money-getter, with extraordinary intellectual capacities. But the moral and spiritual qualities of the previous Bacon would also have to find a field in which their energies could expand themselves. Devachan is such a field.

Hence, the writer goes on, all his plans for moral reform, of research into the abstract principles of nature, all his divine aspirations would find their fruition in Devachan, 'the abode of the Gods', and the entity previously known as Bacon would, in a dream-like state of consciousness, digest all previous experience 'until Karma is satisfied in that direction, the ripple of force reaches the edge of the cyclic basin, and the being moves into the next area of causes', i.e., the next rebirth.

This alternation of states of consciousness, objective in the body and subjective out of it, has been poetically described as a string of black and white beads alternating, strung on the thread of life. But while it is in the subjective state the brooding soul, wrapped in the process of digesting past experience, can never descend to earthly consciousness, and those who wish to communicate with the 'dead' can only do so by ascending in consciousness to the exalted realm of mind in which they dream. In time, after a period which may cover hundreds of years, the hand of Karma begins to draw the dreamer back to waking consciousness. Desire for fresh experience, choosing a body and other environment according to its needs, impels these higher vehicles of the evolving man to assume fresh worldly garments, and so the pilgrim wakes on earth to new discovery and a new-old treading of the Way.

> . . . As when one layeth
> His worn-out robes away,
> And, taking new ones, sayeth,
> 'These will I wear to-day!'
> So putteth by the spirit
> Lightly its garb of flesh,
> And passeth to inherit
> A residence afresh.[1]

[1] *The Song Celestial*, Edwin Arnold.

81

Rebirth

No Rebirth in Animals

The birth may be in the lowest savage or in a prince of virtue, but it will not be in anything less. The degraded belief in rebirth in animal form can be shown to be another example of a spiritual truth misunderstood.

It is all a coarse symbol caricaturing the inner vital truth of reincarnation [says Mr Walker, who studied the subject closely], springing from the striking resemblance between men and animals in feature and dispostion, in voice and mien.[1]

Once consciousness attains to human level there is no return. If evil reaches a stage beyond redemption there may be an utter dissolution of that entity; otherwise, though man may become a super-man, he will never be less than man.

Objections to Rebirth

There are various objections put forward to belief in the doctrine of Rebirth, and they are always the same. The first is that we do not remember previous lives. The answer is simple, that the brain is new each life. Memory is a faculty of the mind, not of the brain which is its temporary instrument, and memory is the power to re-read the indelible records made by every thought and deed in the atmosphere around us. In some way nature preserves in the *akasha*, the substance of manifestation in its finest form, a record which may be accurately 'read'

[1] *Reincarnation.*

82

by those whose spiritual powers have been developed, and it is by this power to contact the Akashic Records that the Buddha, for example, could describe at length the details of his own past lives. But though the average person remembers nothing of the past, there are thousands who, through a lower psychic development, occasionally recall their own past lives and speak of it. But the psychic world in which these chance impressions are picked up by the receptive mind is a world of illusion. Only the trained disciple of a master of nature's forces can speak with accuracy of these things, and it would be part of his training not only 'to dare' and 'to do' but also 'to keep silent'. Moreover, few of those who complain that they do not remember would be brave enough to do so were they suddenly given the power.

The obscuring of memory [writes Owen Rutter] is surely merciful. The remembrance of all the wrongs we have done and all the wrongs which have been done to us, throughout our chain of lives, would be an intolerable burden. Most of us have enough to contend with in this life without burdening ourselves with the recollection of the dangers, the fears and the hates of other lives.[1]

All that we hate and despise in the acts of others we ourselves have sometime done, and paid for, or are paying now. Would it help our present striving up the mountain side to learn of the loathsome acts and thoughts and feelings of our own dead selves? The Law is wise, and it

[1] *The Scales of Karma.*

is well that the brain, the newly created instrument of each rebirth, has only its present folly to remember. As it is, we remember but a tithe of the last week's happenings, and only a thousandth part of the year before. The inner mind is garnering all the time what it needs of the lessons of experience, and the wise man knows that though it is sometimes right to remember, it is often wise to forget.

The second objection usually raised is the injustice of our suffering for the deeds of someone about whom we remember nothing. The answer is the same. It is the inner mind, the reincarnating entity, which draws from the universal memory the lessons it would learn. The man who has forgotten, the man who complains is, though he has a new brain, the man whose deeds he suffers, *is* the Karma of which he now complains. The third objection is that Rebirth is disproved by the doctrine of heredity. This, of course, ignores the difference between the mind that uses the body and the body produced by its parents' union. The former chooses a body, in the sense that it is drawn by the laws of attraction to that body which is suitable to the working out of its Dharma, its Karma for that birth. The body obeys the laws of heredity, of the rebirth of the body; the mind obeys the Law of Karma-Rebirth, of the rebirth of the 'soul'.

Finally, the objection is often raised that the doctrine is uncongenial. 'I don't *want* to come back to this world of misery and toil,' the complainer says. The Law replies, 'Who cares about your likes and dislikes, you who claim to be separate? In essence you are part of the Law, and made it so.' If a brick falls on my head I may dislike the law of gravity, but I don't deny that it exists. And why this fierce objection to return? He who understands the Law knows that all causes have effects, and that all effects have sprung from causes. The deeds of the past must be 'digested'. Where? The obvious and reasonable answer is here, on earth, and if the sufferer dislikes this life it is he who made it so.

VII

Who believes in Karma and Rebirth?

Schopenhauer said that if an Asiatic asked him for a
definition of Europe he would answer that it was that
part of the world which was haunted by the incredible
delusion that man's present birth was his first entrance
into life. Taking the world as a whole, therefore, it
would almost be justifiable to reverse the question at the
head of this chapter, and to ask, Who does not accept the
Law of Karma-Rebirth, and on what grounds do they
reject it? In any event, it is pertinent to examine the Euro-
pean attitude to the doctrine, and most books on the
subject give, with a wealth of detail and quotation, the
evidence which shows how widespread such belief has
become. On the other hand, as Owen Rutter points out:

No one is likely to accept a philosophy which does not appeal
to him, nor is he necessarily to be convinced of its truth,
because, throughout the ages, men of intelligence have
accepted it. Nevertheless, although few people are influenced
by argument, many are glad to listen to explanation,[1]

especially when that explanation of life's inequalities and
suffering is the only one which accords with reason and

[1] *The Scales of Karma.*

experience. In his interesting introduction to *Reincarnation*, E. D. Walker proves how

once the whole civilized world embraced reincarnation, and found therein a complete answer to that riddle of man's descent and destiny which the inexorable sphinx, Life, propounds to every traveller along her way. But the Western Branch of the race, in working out the material conquest of the world, has acquired the compensating discontent of a material philosophy. It has lost the old faith and drifted into a shadowy region, where the eagerness for 'practical' things rejects whatever cannot be physically proven.

Yet scores of enlightened thinkers and most poets have seen, with spiritual certainty, the truth of a Law which the State religion has expelled in favour of dogmas unknown to its Founder, and none has yet disproved their ever new 'discovery'.

The East has known the Law from time immemorial; the West accepted it until and for a long time after the birth of Christianity. Greek and Roman, Egyptian and Jew, in one form or another knew the Law, and chapters of books and books themselves have been written to show its prevalence in the days of Jesus, and the Master's adoption without question of the Law in which he had been bred. On Karma, the Master said: 'By their fruits ye shall know them. Do men gather grapes of thorns, or figs of thistles? Even so every good tree bringeth forth good fruit; but the corrupt tree bringeth forth evil fruit. A good tree cannot bring forth evil fruit, neither can a corrupt tree bring forth good fruit.' And he who rewards accordingly is no Being, however mighty, but the Father within, the Buddha within, the SELF within from which has evolved both man and the all-embracing Law. On Rebirth, Jesus said, when asked about the man born blind, that it was neither he that had sinned nor his parents. Clearly it was he in a previous life. And whence the widely current rumours that John the Baptist was Elias, 'which was for to come again'?

But, it may be said, the ancients were ignorant of the truth before the coming of Christ, and a few Biblical passages may be incorrectly reported. It is strange, then, that so many writers, in prose and verse, in the last three hundred years have apparently seen the inevitability of the doctrine. From Wordsworth's famous *Ode on the Intimations of Immortality* to Edwin Arnold's splendid Eighth Book of the *Light of Asia*, English poetry is filled with allusions to the Law, and the writers in prose were never far behind. Some write as if homesick for a land they feel as 'home'. In many cases this is the East, and they are therefore ill at ease in what to them is an alien Western body. Others are not so certain where they were previously born. But 'memory appears to be a palimpsest from which nothing is ever obliterated', declared Professor Dixon, and many a poet has felt convincingly that he or she has lived before.

> Perhaps I lived before
> In some strange world where first my soul

And all this passionate love was shaped, and joy, and pain
That come, I know not whence, and sway my deeds
Are old imperious memories, blind yet strong,
That this world stirs within me.[1]

Shakespeare made rational enquiry in Sonnet LIX;

If there be nothing new, but that which is
Hath been before, how are our brains beguil'd
Which, labouring for invention, bear amiss
The second burthen of a former child!

Tennyson, more mystical, in a little-known sonnet begins:

As when with downcast eyes we muse and brood
And ebb into a former life, or seem
To lapse far back in a confused dream
To states of mystical similitude . . .

Browning is more personal, in a poem to Evelyn Hope,
who died at the age of sixteen:

Just because I was twice as old
And our paths in the world diverged so wide,
Each was naught to each, must I be told?
We were fellow mortals, naught beside?

And he answers his own enquiry:

I claim you still, for my own love's sake!
Delayed it may be for more lives yet,
Through worlds I shall traverse, not a few;
Much is to learn and much to forget
Ere the time be come for taking you.

[1] George Eliot in *The Spanish Gypsy*.

And Tennyson, later in the sonnet above quoted:

> So friend, when first I looked upon your face,
> Our thoughts gave answer each to each, so true
> Opposed mirrors each reflecting each,
> Although I knew not in what time or place
> Methought that I had often met with you,
> And each had lived in others' mind and speech.

Rossetti remembered places:

> I have been here before,
>   But where or how I cannot tell;
> I know the grass beyond the door,
>   The sweet, keen smell,
> The sighing sound; the lights around the shore.

> You have been mine before,
>   How long ago I may not know;
> But just when at that swallow's soar
>   Your neck turned so,
> Some veil did fall—I knew it all of yore.

In *Lalla Rookh*, Thomas Moore likened the spirit passing from body to body to a lighted brand passing from hand to hand until it reached the goal, a remarkable echo of the Eastern analogy of the candle-flame or the wave to describe the re-incarnating entity that moves from life to life on the long road to perfection.

But it has been left to John Masefield, the present Poet Laureate, himself a student of Buddhism, to proclaim his personal creed for all to hear:

John Masefield on Rebirth

I hold that when a person dies
His soul returns again to earth;
Arrayed in some new flesh-disguise,
Another mother gives him birth.
With sturdier limbs and brighter brain
The old soul takes the road again . . .
So shall I fight, so shall I tread,
In this long war beneath the stars;
So shall a glory wreathe my head,
So shall I faint and show the scars,
Until this case, this clogging mould,
Be smithied all to kingly gold.

The list is endless. For those who like precedent for their own belief there is ample precedent, and any man who for the moment doubts the truth of a doctrine which seems to run counter to so much of the popular belief around him may take heart of courage from the fact that so many of those who have given the matter thought have been impressed with the reasonableness, even the inevitability of the Law.

VIII

Karma and Rebirth applied

It has been said that a man believes a doctrine when he behaves as if it were true. Assuming, then, that for a while one were to behave as if the Law of Karma *were* the all-embracing Law, and that life, instead of a span of a few minutes to seventy odd years, were an endless series of days and nights, days of labour and nights of rest, wherein each fragment-mind of the Essence of Mind was slowly learning the only lesson, to become what it is— assume this for a while, and consider the result on character.

The SELF is One; it IS; and Karma is its Law:

Never the spirit was born; the spirit shall cease to be never;
  Never was time it was not; End and Beginning are dreams!
Birthless and deathless and changeless remaineth the spirit for ever;
  Death has not touched it at all, dead though the house of it seems!

Such is the answer of the *Bhagavad Gita* to those who believe that life can die. There is no death.

If this be true, the effect is immediate and tremendous. Each man learns that he is and always has been master of his future, the captain of his soul. He knows, in the words

of the *Dhammapada*, 'By oneself the evil is done, by oneself one suffers; by oneself the evil is left undone, by oneself one is purified. Purity and impurity belong to
oneself; no one can purify another.' But he knows, too,
that 'Self is the lord of self', and that he must therefore
curb himself 'as the merchant curbs a good horse'.
Henceforth he is master of himself as well as of his destiny.
For him there is no more drifting, as a rudderless ship.
He knows that all that pertains to the separative self is
evil, that all that pertains to the larger Self, his truer self,
is proportionately good. He must choose, for 'the cycle
of necessity' is not a circle but a spiral, and the path goes
up or down. Henceforth the pilgrim chooses his own
journey, and though there will always be guides available,
he must learn to travel alone. 'You yourself must make
the effort,' says the *Dhammapada*, 'Buddhas do but point
the Way.' And again, in *The Voice of the Silence*, 'Prepare
thyself, for thou wilt have to travel on alone. The
Teacher can but point the Way. The Path is one for all;
the means to reach the goal must vary with the Pilgrims.'
Yet now there is a joyous sense of the community of
souls, the Oneness of all forms of life, the pilgrimage of
the homeless making their slow way home.

Character-building

For the first time there is encouragement to deliberate
character-building, a thoughtful planning of the future
without regard to time. 'Sow a thought and you reap an

act; sow an act and you reap a habit; sow a habit and you reap a character; sow a character and you reap a destiny.' So runs the old rune, and it is now seen to be true. Are you tired of a peevish temper? Seek its cause and remove the cause. Would you have greater concentration of mind? None can prevent it, if you have the will to prepare a plan for self-development and to carry it through.

When a man accepts and partially understands the working of Karma, he can at once begin this building of character, setting each stone with deliberate care, knowing that he is building for Eternity. There is no longer hasty running up and pulling down, working on one plan to-day, on another to-morrow, on none at all the day after; but there is the drafting of a well-thought-out scheme of character, as it were, and then the building according to the scheme, for the Soul becomes an architect as well as a builder, and wastes no more time in abortive beginnings.[1]

All this takes time, but there is time for patience, both for the total of work to be done and for waiting for the right and proper moment for each act. On the one hand, 'drop by drop is the water-pot filled', whether with good or evil; on the other hand, there is a rhythm in events, a 'tide in the affairs of men' which all should study and use.

To act and act wisely when the time for action comes, to wait and wait patiently when it is time for repose, puts man in accord with the rising and falling tides, so that, with nature

[1] *Karma*, Annie Besant.

and law at his back, and truth and beneficence as his beacon light, he may accomplish wonders.[1]

Note that the beacon light is composed of truth and beneficence, understanding and compassion. The Buddha was known as the All-Enlightened One, but also as the All-Compassionate One. There can be no true love without understanding, for understanding of man's integrity gives birth to that benevolence and beneficence which comes with a vision of THAT. On the other hand, there can be no true understanding without love. The mind knows more and more *about* the objects of its survey. Love knows. Thereafter life is sacred and one's brother is oneself. 'He who looks into the pupil of his brother's eye sees himself; he who sees the Self in all and all in the Self—he will not injure the Self by the Self.' Or to return once more to *The Voice of the Silence*:

Thou shalt not separate thy being from BEING and the rest, but merge the Ocean in the drop, the drop within the Ocean. So shalt thou be in full accord with all that lives, bear love to men as though they were thy brother-pupils, disciples of one Teacher, the sons of one sweet mother.

In brief, he who applies the Law to daily life will find that so far from being cold, or leading to heartlessness, the Law of Harmony and Justice is equally the Law of Love.

[1] *Practical Occultism*, H. P. Blavatsky.

Karma and Rebirth Applied

Changing Values

An understanding of the Law leads to a greater understanding of our own and others' suffering. Great events are seen as of small importance, and the littlest act is seen as the possible parent of great consequences. With a growing sense of responsibility for every thought and act there comes a new valuation of all circumstance. There is a greater willingness to face facts as they are and a reluctance to label them. Things and events are seen as neither good nor bad; they are. It is man who adds the changing labels to the bare events. The value of intense sincerity is obvious, for if to lie to others is evil, to lie to oneself is an absolute barrier on the Way. Even sin is the less sinful when it stands alone, and is not aggravated by self-delusion as to what it is. In the delightful words of Gerald Gould:

> For God's sake, if you sin, take pleasure in it,
>   And do it for the pleasure. Do not say:
> 'Behold the spirit's liberty!—a minute
>   Will see the earthly vesture break away
> And God shine through.' Say: 'Here's a sin—I'll sin it;
>   And there's the price of sinning—and I'll pay!'

In the same way, happiness is seen for what it is. Most men would say that it was the aim of life, yet, as I wrote elsewhere,

when the conception is analysed, it is found to contain at least four ingredients, of which the first is a sense of security. In

96

the second place there must be an absence of worry, which to most men means an absence of that fruitful cause of worry, responsibility. Thirdly, there must be an absence of strife, or conflict; and fourthly, there is a powerful sense of comfort, involving a 'comfortable' income, good health, a happy home. . . . Such a conception is a lie, utterly selfish, and impossible of achievement.[1]

Even when such an animal contentment is for a short while achieved it is only at the expense of utter forgetfulness of the intolerable misery of millions of mankind. Not that pleasure is evil, nor happiness a sin, but to seek for it, to make it the motive of life and the goal of all endeavour, is a low, unworthy motive for treading the Way.

It is more, it is undignified, and one of the first effects of applying the Law to all one's actions is a new-found sense of dignity. Man is no longer a pawn on a chessboard, moved by an unseen Hand, nor a blown leaf on the winds of destiny. He is the patient reaper of his self-sown past, and the deliberate creator not only of such future as may be built by the right user of all opportunities, but the creator of opportunity which may be rightly used. The wise man uses Karma as the scientist uses electricity, and the Law is just as impersonal. He who is ignorant of its powers or careless in its handling will suffer accordingly, and only himself may bear the blame, though others may suffer for his folly. Again, if a man uses a natural law to

[1] From a speech reported in *Buddhism in England*, for July, 1938.

a selfish end it will work as well as if the end were sheer benevolence. He who wants will get; it does not follow that having got it he will be satisfied with what he has got. There is such a thing as dust and ashes, and he who sows for himself will reap unhappiness.

Few men are their own masters in business; the vast majority have their outward lives planned for them. Yet in the inner life all are equally free. There is dignity in the thought of a long-term planning for the development of character. In one life much may be done, but in endless lives to come, as many as are needed, all is possible, all will assuredly be done.

Only in action will the wisdom come. Lead the life, and the Way will open and the truth be finally attained. Such is the Wisdom in all Scriptures, but the Way, the Middle Way of harmony, must be trodden for the sake of the SELF, and not for the self alone. Mistakes are inevitable, but he who is willing to learn will pay the price demanded, retrace his steps to the point of divergence, and march on. And he will learn from his own mistakes to be less critical of others. Where those he despises stand at the moment, he once stood, even as he will stand where now, on the heights ahead of him, he sees the more developed of his fellow men. The parable of the mote and the beam is always apt, and it is to be found in the *Dhammapada* of Buddhism, in Indian philosophy, and in most of the religions of the world. In the *Dhammapada* it reads, 'The fault of others is easily perceived, but that of oneself is difficult to perceive; the faults of others one lays open to all, but one's own one hides, as a cheat will hide the bad die from the gambler.'

Mistakes will be made, and be paid for, in valuations as in all else. For values pertain to the mind, not to things, and as the mind evolves, so must its values and its power to value wisely. Sin and happiness must be re-valued, as already shown; so must time, for it is only time which separates those below us in the scale of evolution and those ahead. So must death and the fear of death. When the body is seen as a garment of the soul, and the soul or returning Self is found to be one with the SELF, where is the sorrow at the need of sleep, of rest at the close of day? Again, a lesson well learnt can never be bought too dearly, and many of those who in the stress of war have lost their all—visible belongings—have learnt, as only the violent teacher, war, has been able to teach them, the unimportance of possessions, when all that a man possesses is what he is.

The way is a Middle Way, a path of temperance, of the due avoidance of extremes. 'All opposites provoke their opposites', which is another way of saying that action and reaction are equal and opposite. All extremes must ultimately cancel out, even as a pendulum, however fiercely swung, will finally fall to rest. The more a spring is compressed, the greater will be the recoil. The Middle Way avoids extremes, and threads its way between the opposites so lightly and so reasonably that no act is followed by reaction, and hence there is no need for a Self to suffer the consequences of the act. 'The perfect act has no result.'

But the Middle Way has nought to do with compromise, where compromise means loosing the reins of principle. That which is right, for that individual at that time in those circumstances, is right; all other act is wrong. The way between two extremes is not a little of each, but a third way, the genuine Middle Way which is not so much between the opposites as a strait and narrow way, 'narrow as a razor's edge', between yet above them both. If an act is right, it is neither too much this nor that; if it is not right it has slipped down the steeps of illusion on one side or the other. And all the while the winds of doubt are blowing, cold and keen. . . .

The road is long, and the pilgrim soon grows weary. The accumulated Karma of the past, which in its own inexorable time will offer itself for cancelling, is appalling in the true sense of the word. Habits of thought and act and motive must be halted and reversed; all values changed. We must 'cease to do evil' before we can 'learn to do good'. Then, when the trend of our acts is purified, we must 'cleanse the heart', till the 'I' which is not I has learnt that it is of the Essence of Pure Mind.

According to Yoga, the Indian science of spiritual development, there are many branches of the Way, of which three may be mentioned in particular. Jnana Yoga is the way of Knowledge, an ever-increasing understanding as the awakening faculty of Buddhi, the intuition, illumines the mind. Bhakti Yoga is the way of devotion, of love, of utter self-sacrifice in the service of the Beloved Ideal. The third is Karma Yoga, and this, it would seem, is the Dharma, the present duty or right path for the West. This is the way of Action, of the right performance of all duty, however high, however small. Yet Jnana and Karma Yoga are complementary. On the Middle Way

action and vision go hand in hand, and that is why the teachings of the Gita alternate between knowledge and action in a way so baffling to the purely intellectual man. Purified and disciplined action opens the inner eye and grants the vision of the highest that the disciple is yet capable of seeing. But that vision must not remain a mere private ecstasy. It must be translated into action, and so built into the personality before another range of vision can present itself to the inner eye and the way be opened for yet another cyclic advance.[1]

The burden of Karma is heavy. All alike have heavy debts to pay. Yet none, so the Wisdom teaches, is ever faced with more than he can bear. Whether or not we can grin, we must bear it, and it is folly to attempt to run away. Yet thousands believe that by moving their bodies across the world they will escape from Karma. Others, equally foolish, believe that they can escape from 'the

[1] *The Yoga of the Bhagavad Gita*, Sri Krishna Prem.

whips and scorns of time' by suicide. Only the body dies; the Karma remains, with the added burden of self-murder and the weakling will that feared to pay. Others, as all psychologists know, 'escape' into neuroses, often attaining the degree of madness, believing that in their own minds they will escape from the harshness of the world without; others again, like the proverbial ostrich, seek to escape by pretending that, as they cannot see the doom approaching, it is not there. Their efforts are vain. As a gentleman pays his debts, so a Karmically educated gentleman invites the bill and pays it willingly.

Here, however, a curious minor law asserts itself. It seems to be that he who deliberately takes himself in hand, and sets about the task of his own self-development, calls down on himself a larger share of 'suspended' Karma than otherwise he would have had to endure. The price of entry on the Path with open eyes, it seems, is an immediate testing, self-demanded; and many a student, finding the reward of incipient effort to be, not as he hoped a sense of spiritual well-being but a host of trials and obstacles, gives up the attempt, and joins once more the army of drifters who, with no higher goal than personal happiness, form the bulk of mankind. Those who survive these apparent testings find themselves at the entrance to a Path whose end is self-Enlightenment, and on this Path, 'the first step is to live to benefit mankind'. In a message to the American Theosophists in 1889 H. P. Blavatsky quoted a Master of the Wisdom as saying,

Assuming Others' Karma

The Universe groans under the weight of Karma, and none other than self-sacrificial Karma relieves it. How many of you have helped humanity to carry its smallest burden, that you should all regard yourselves as Theosophists? Oh, men of the West, who would play at being the Saviours of mankind before they even spare the life of a mosquito whose sting threatens them! would you be partakers of Divine Wisdom or true Theosophists? Then do as the gods when incarnated do. Feel yourselves the vehicles of the whole humanity, mankind as part of yourselves, and act accordingly.

IX

The Ending of Karma and Rebirth

Even if modern science and modern Christianity are gravely at variance, the leading scientists of the day are rediscovering the truths of the Wisdom which is older than any religion. Sir James Jeans, in *The Mysterious Universe*, has written: 'The universe can best be pictured . . . as consisting of pure thought', and that 'its creation must have been an act of thought'. This is pure Vedanta and pure Buddhism, and it is the basis of Theosophy. The Essence of Mind, as the Patriarch Wei Lang described it, the Universal Mind of modern philosophy, is 'intrinsically pure', and each of our human minds is an outpost of that 'cosmic consciousness'. What is the relation between the two? 'Thou *art* THAT,' says the Wisdom of India. 'Look within, thou *art* Buddha,' says the numerically largest religion in the world. Man is enlightened but knows it not. 'I and my Father are one,' said Christ, the Christos or 'God within' of every man. The difference between an enlightened and an unenlightened man is only this, said Wei Lang, that one knows it and the other does not. But between the two states of consciousness there lies a Way, a long and weary way from the might-be to the has-become, a way of becoming until the littlest blade of grass has entered Buddhahood, until each living thing has re-become what it potentially is, the All.

Potentially we are one with the Absolute.

But having fallen into illusion we have the experience of a separated life which is not terminated at death. We remain in the illusion until we have exhausted it, until we have learned the full significance of our deeds, and remoulded them so that a return to the identity-consciousness is possible; for works are a means to knowledge, and knowledge the means to liberation. Thus karma-reincarnation is alike the machinery of the illusion and the escapement from it.[1]

But if the nature of man is determined by his user of the Law, so that in a very real sense he *is* his Karma, and if every act and thought is adding to the total of cause-effects, how will it end? According to the Wisdom the answer to this question, as to most others of its kind, is a paradox, that none may know the ending until he has reached the end. Only he who has 'exhausted' his Karma may utterly know the Law. How, then, is the unen-lightened mortal to proceed? The answer seems to be, in Christian terminology, with faith and works. There must be faith in the Law that the due performance of all duty will in some mysterious way remove one from the sway of Karma, and faith is not, as a humorist put it, believing what you know to be untrue, but knowing with a partially awakened intuition the truth of a law which the

[1] *Mysticism of East and West*, Loftus Hare.

intellect has not as yet been able to grasp. In this sense only is faith of value, as an inner conviction that where the finger of the guide is pointing there is a way, the right Way to the goal desired. But faith is valueless unless it be expressed in works. We in the West are an action-loving people, and even in the more introverted Indian mind there is an equal necessity for the knowledge within to appear in acts without, even as the Universe itself 'becomes itself' by manifesting outwardly.

But action, right or wrong, alike produces fresh results. Where, then, is the end, if even the due performance of all duty brings us back again to reap the harvest, still the victim of our own endeavour, still on the Wheel of Rebirth, bound on the cycle of our own necessity? The answer is twofold and yet one. By removing the self which causes and is its Karma, and by acting so dispassionately, so 'resultlessly', that every act is without reaction, and therefore needs no actor to suffer the consequences, good or evil, of the act.

There are two ways to the Goal, to diminish the self, the power of the personality, until it is servant to the Self, and then to diminish the Self, the 'soul' or character, until it ceases to have any will or purpose other than that of the SELF, or the Vedantin rather than the Buddhist way, to increase the power of the SELF in the Self, and then in the self till the separative impulse has ceased to exist and the whole of the man is One. In this connection it has been said that all men serve a self, but their enlightenment depends on the size of the self they serve. It is the purely selfish lust of the egotist, the more enlightened love of family and neighbour and the immediate commonweal, or is it a love, an enlightened and illumined love for all mankind? As is the answer, so will be the attainment of that individual in the process of becoming.

The first answer, then, to the problem of the ending of Karma is that the self which causes and must suffer Karma must be left to die. When the three fires of hatred, lust and illusion die for want of fuelling, the personality, robbed of its independent willing, becomes the obedient servant of the soul, and as the soul gives up its life it learns to live. For the only slavery is desire, and he who learns to let go, to climb the wind-swept hills of self-becoming, naked of all possessions and desire, will drink the mountain air of freedom, and find the peace that lies not in the satisfaction but in the controlling of desire.

The second answer is twin to the first. 'Without attachment, constantly perform action which is duty, for performing action without attachment man verily reacheth the Supreme.' So runs the *Bhagavad Gita*, and its theme is the absence of attachment to the act. There must be no more action in which 'I' strive for a result. But if the act seem good, that is, to be duty and no more, let there be the performing of that action, regardless of the consequence.

Whose acts are free from the moulding of desire, whose acts are burned up by the fire of wisdom, he is called Sage by the wise. Having abandoned all attachment to the fruits of action, ever content, seeking refuge in none, while doing acts he is not doing anything. Free from desire, his thoughts controlled by the SELF, having abandoned all attachment, performing action by the body alone, he commits no sin. Content with what he receives, free from the pairs of opposites, without envy, balanced in success and failure, though he has acted he is not bound. For with all attachments dead, harmonious, his thoughts established in wisdom, his work as sacrifices, all his actions melt away.

The secret, then, is motive. Action must go on, for only by right action can the Law be used to its own ending. But the motive for each act must be increasingly selfless until all that we once thought I, and such a splendid I, is seen to be dross and purged away. Thereafter there is a doing of the deed that must be done, and the doer's motive is merely that, being right, it should be done. It must be noted that such action has become 'right' in the highest sense, by being that which should be done. So long as the thought of self remains, a good deed binds the doer as much as any sin. If I am generous, with the thought of how generous I am, the results will be good, but I must return to receive them. Only when each act is a cheerful, unattached performance of 'right action' is the doer free. As is said in *Light on the Path*, 'Desire to sow no seed for your own harvesting; desire only to sow that seed the fruit of which shall feed the world.' Otherwise, 'Verily, Brethren, there is no end to the suffering of beings buried in blindness who, seized by craving, are brought again and again to birth unceasingly.'[1]

The Buddhism of the Northern School, the Mahayana or Great Vehicle, has developed a lovely doctrine of the Bodhisattva, one who having attained Enlightenment works on for humanity, guarding him so far as the Law permits from folly, guiding him with a finger pointing the Way. These great ones of all religions, variously known as Arhats, Bodhisattvas, Rishis, Mahatmas, Masters, Saints and Brothers, form collectively, the Wisdom tells, a guardian wall about humanity, and watch its progress with a troubled eye. For though each has reached the end of his own immediate journey and attained his own Release, yet he may not 'interfere' with another's Karma, nor would it help him if he could. From the beginning to the end of the journey man must travel alone, but he travels guarded, guided and in some way protected from his folly, and it is the aim of the noblest of mankind to add to that Guardian Wall. When the weary but triumphant Pilgrim nears the end of the journey, and the gates of Enlightenment swing wide to receive him with his due reward, Compassion speaks and says: 'Can there be bliss when all that lives must suffer? Shalt thou be saved and hear the whole world cry?'[2] And he who after a thousand lives of fierce endeavour has achieved self-mastery abandons all that he had striven to

[1] *Samyutta Nikaya.*
[2] *The Voice of the Silence.*

obtain, forgoes the guerdon of his efforts, and returns and by his great Renunciation hastens the liberation of all mankind. Yet this too is the Law, for the Law is Justice, but the Law is also Love.

There are those who seek the SELF by learning; those who seek it by devotion to the Beloved Ideal; those who seek by the way of action. There is the path of Occultism, of the science of the spiritual forces which rule mankind; there is the way of Mysticism, of a vision of the Goal whereby all else is seen as insignificant; there is the way of Zen, that thrusts aside all obstacles and marches, not up the gentler paths of slow endeavour, but straightway up the hill. All these are ways within the Way, for 'the ways to the One are as many as the lives of men', and each before he treads the Path must in truth become the Path, for the Life and the Truth and the Way are One, even as Karma uses and is used by all impartially. Karma is truth and the way to truth; Karma is justice and therefore uses the illusion of time. But Karma is also love, for 'Love is the fulfilling of the Law'.